Authentic Christianity

Authentic Christianity

Richard Taylor

New Wine Press

New Wine Ministries
PO Box 17
Chichester
West Sussex
United Kingdom
PO19 2AW

Copyright © 2009 Richard Taylor

All rights reserved. No part of this publication may be reproduced, stored in a retrieval system, or transmitted in any form or by any means, electronic, mechanical, photocopying or otherwise, without the prior written consent of the publisher. Short extracts may be used for review purposes.

Scripture quotations are taken from the following version of the Bible:
New King James Version (NKJV). Copyright © 1982 by
Thomas Nelson, Inc
King James Version. Crown copyright.

ISBN 978-1-905991-47-1

Typeset by **documen**, www.documen.co.uk
Cover design by CCD, www.ccdgroup.co.uk
Printed in Malta

Contents

	Introduction	7
Chapter 1	The Losses in the Garden	11
Chapter 2	Choices	31
Chapter 3	Hallmarks of an Authentic Christian	49
Chapter 4	Four Lies of Discouragement	63
Chapter 5	Faith into Action	75
Chapter 6	Being a Blessing	87
Chapter 7	Authentic or Synthetic Christianity?	99
	About the author	111

Introduction

Over the years the Christian Church has been subjected to hearing all kinds of nonsense from various pulpits, conferences, television, books and CDs. This has been filled with the opinions of others and mistaken as doctrinal statements, creating ideologies without an authentic hallmark of Christianity upon them. The resulting hype, hysteria and sensationalism of these ideas have caused many people to want more and more of these types of experiences because it often helps them to feel good. And yet we find that Jesus never preached a feel good factor Gospel. He never said to disciples, "Whatever you want, you can have." He preached sacrifice, self-denial and humility. Jesus said to His disciples,

"If anyone desires to come after Me, let him deny himself, and take up his cross, and follow Me."
(Matthew 16:24)

This is the true, authentic Gospel.

One of the things I'm deeply concerned about by this is that many people are chasing sensationalism over the scriptural. A major problem with this is that these same people then base their Christian experience, their whole faith, upon what is demonstrative. They believe that God's Spirit has to *do* something to them to make them feel good. This is something that is being sought by many around the world, leaving them chasing after blessings and chasing after anointing.

When the sensational is pursued it results in anointing often being elevated and promoted above doctrine. But anointing will always be subservient to the Word of God, and the Bible should be the benchmark by which we measure everything. Scripture warns us that in the last days many will come and say that they are the Christ, the meaning of this word being "Anointed One". But Jesus warns us very explicitly not to be deceived because many will come with "anointings". He said to his disciples,

> *"Take heed that no one deceives you. For many will come in My name, saying, 'I am the Christ,' and will deceive many."*
> (Matthew 24:4-5)

As authentic Christians we must listen to the warning from Jesus that this kind of deception is inevitable. Looking at the same chapter of the Bible we find that Jesus also says,

> *"Then many false prophets will rise up and deceive many. And because lawlessness will abound, the love of many will grow cold. But he who endures to the end shall be saved. And this gospel of the kingdom will be preached in all the world as a witness to all the nations, and then the end will come."*
> (Matthew 24:11-14)

Never forget that miracles do not authenticate who God is. The occult practices miracles, as do many cults. When Moses went to Pharaoh he took his staff, threw it to the floor and it turned into a snake but we must also remember though that the sorcerers came and did exactly the same. We have to understand that in the last days even the Antichrist will perform signs, wonders and miracles. Just look in the Bible to understand this.

Authentic Christians are those who respond to the claims of Jesus Christ, not necessarily those who are perceived as being spiritual doing wacky and wonderful things in the name of the Holy Spirit. What is the Holy Spirit for? The Spirit has come to reveal truth and to glorify Jesus as found in the Book of John:

"But when he, the Spirit of truth, comes, he will guide you into all truth. He will not speak on his own; he will speak only what he hears, and he will tell you what is yet to come. He will bring glory to me by taking from what is mine and making it known to you."

(John 16:13-14 NIV)

I find it hard to find much at the moment that's done in the name of the Holy Spirit which brings glory to Jesus. Instead, I find more being done solely to bring attention to individuals. What concerns me is that we throw Scripture to one side at the expense of experientialism and believe that by supernatural or incredible super knowledge we can attain salvation.

Take note of this: you do not have to go to anybody else to get what God wants to give you because you can go directly yourself. So, we must always base manifestations, experiences of the Spirit and what God is doing in the Christian Church, upon the Word of God. Remember, there is only one mediator between man and God and His name is Jesus Christ.

We need to stop and look at Scripture to check the authenticity of any genuine move of God. I like to use the Bible as an acronym to remind myself of what it really is:

Basic **I**nstructions **B**efore **L**eaving **E**arth. God gave us this book to educate us and to help us to be mature in understanding His nature and how He works in and through us, through the world and through the Christian Church. The Bible is the very thing by which we must always measure everything that claims to be of God.

Throughout history no person has sparked as much controversy as Jesus Christ. He is either adored or abhorred, loved or loathed, revered or rebuked and people continually misconceive, misjudge and malign Him. With so many differing opinions put forward it is no wonder that what it really means to be a follower of Christ is often lost, waylaid or misinterpreted.

So this book aims to explore authentic Christianity. It looks at what it really means to be a follower of Christ and explores the hallmarks of a genuine follower of Christ. Together, let us look to the evidence of the Word of God, our final authority, for truth and understanding in finding practical ways to demonstrate the love of God to those who need it.

Richard Taylor

CHAPTER 1

The Losses in the Garden

Too many Christians are hanging on by their fingernails, coming to church for an hour a week and thinking that this is all there is – that church is all about worship meetings, home groups, paying your tithe and going home with a warm glow. But that is because many believers have subscribed to a feel-good brand of church that has little to do with New Testament Christianity.

> **"Authentic Christianity is about knowing who you are in Christ, what your function is in the Body of Christ, and understanding how to serve God in the place where He has put you."**

Instead, the real purpose of attending church is to be equipped for the work of the ministry that will take place when we leave the safe confines of the church building. But even then, we cannot expect our church leaders to somehow be the answer to every problem we've got and the solution to our every need. God has placed in the Church the gifts of evangelists, teachers, prophets and pastors, so that they can equip *us to do the work of the ministry*. The church leaders' function to is to equip *and release* the Body to minister to others. Because in so many places we find this isn't happening in our nation, it's time to redress the situation. Every one of us has got to take ownership and responsibility for the lives we're living, where we are living them, and resolve that we will live them to the glory of God.

Authentic Christianity is about knowing who you are in Christ, what your function is in the Body of Christ, and understanding how to serve God in the place where He has put you. At its most basic level it involves, for every one of us, telling others what we really believe about Jesus Christ. We can no longer just rely on preachers, pastors of the church or "special" ministries to do this for us. Every one of us has got to take up the baton.

We can look at our society and immediately see that it is in a mess. The cause of that mess is not due to whichever political party is in power or due to vocal minority groups who are disrupting the status quo. The finger of blame can only be pointed at sin. Society doesn't like to hear this word – it is too busy dreaming up new reasons why people do bad things: we blame it on bad parenting, social deprivation, lack of education, trauma – anything other than what the Bible describes as the root of all man's problems. But sin is the sickness that pervades society's problems and we will only see society begin to turn around as we commit ourselves to preaching a straightforward Gospel that does not dodge the issue. The Bible reveals the nature and severity of sin in both the Old and New Testament. The prophet Ezekiel wrote that,

"the soul that sins will surely die."

If we fail to preach the revelation of Christ and the need to be cleansed from sin, then we will not see authentic conversions to Christ.

As the Church we often fail to see the importance of preaching the Word of God. Too often we lean on making church an experience of the Spirit and trivialize the teaching of Scripture. The power of the Word must work hand in hand with the power of the Holy Spirit. We can't have one without the other or we are seriously out of balance.

Here is an excerpt from a letter that a friend of mine, George Canty, a gifted preacher and writer, sent to me when I was an associate minister in Solihull. He says:

"The history of this Godless world consists of lurching from one catastrophic situation to the next. The roots of the present criminal trouble is not destitution, we knew what that was, but I say quite categorically that the cause of today's malaise is the loss of the Word of God in the churches where liberalism and critical theories have destroyed biblical authority."

Abraham Lincoln once posed the question to a group of students he was addressing, "If you call a sheep's tail a leg, how many legs will the sheep have?" One of his students answered "five". Of course, the answer will always be four! You can call a tail what you like but it will still be a tail. Similarly, you can call sin whatever you like, but it is still sin. Jesus died for the sin of the world and three days later He rose again from the dead. That is the essence of the message we have been given and if we don't continue to preach this message, society is going to continue to weaken.

Why do we sin?

When we take communion we are reminded that Jesus died for the sins of the world. He died that we might have our souls saved. But more than simply receiving a ticket to

Heaven, Jesus died that we may be transformed into new people – redeemed soul, spirit, body and mind, so that we might become effective agents in His Kingdom.

"Therefore, if anyone is in Christ, he is a new creation; old things have passed away; behold, all things have become new."
(2 Corinthians 5:17)

This is the real power of the shed blood of Christ and is truly authentic Christianity – the fact that a person, however entrenched in sin, can be changed from the inside out to become a "new creation". That does not mean that we instantly stop sinning and become perfect – we know that's not true – but now, sin can no longer exercise the same power over us as before. Sin's power is broken when we surrender our life to Christ.

People "sin" because there is an internal struggle in each of us. We are all born with the "Adamic" nature given to us by our first parents, Adam and Eve. In other words, we are not born innocent and grow up gradually learning how to sin through wrong choices – a theory that scientists and particularly humanists or atheists would have us believe – we are born into sin from the moment we enter this world. As we grow up we just get better at sinning! Psalm 51:5 expresses the real truth of the situation:

"In sin my mother conceived me"

and we know that

"the wages of sin is death"
(Romans 6:23)

In a sense we are struggling with moral dualism in that there are two struggles within every single Christian believer. There is the nature of Christ and there is the old nature of man. The new nature and the old nature are in conflict with one another. This new nature is known as the spirit, the inward man or the new man, whereas the old nature is known as the flesh, the outward man or the old man. You'll have read those terms in Scripture. These are two capacities focused in opposite directions. Your old, pre-conversion nature, gravitates towards evil desires. It is not thinking about godly things and it doesn't want to do them. Your new nature in Christ, however, does desire to do godly things. They are in opposition to each other, hence there will be conflict.

Paul states in Galatians 5:17,

"For the flesh lusts against the Spirit, and the Spirit against the flesh; and these are contrary to one another".

In other words, Paul says, they therefore cannot work together. The struggle we face is how we allow the new nature to become the dominating factor in our lives, which is what we need to do to live a morally good and correct Christian life.

That's harder said than done, it truly is, but that is the nature of our journey and the characteristic of authentic Christianity.

> **"Some of the most intense fighting can be found in the human heart between the flesh and the spirit"**
>
> *James E. Haynes, Jr.*

When a person becomes a Christian, they receive a new nature; the nature of Jesus Christ now lives in that person. Suddenly things take on a whole new meaning. Whereas it was OK to behave in a certain way and commit certain sins without conscience before, suddenly those things are not OK and the Holy Spirit speaks to our conscience and tells us which things are not right. This is the beginning of the conflict, if you will, the "dualism" that we suffer from as our old nature struggles to surrender itself to the will of the new nature. Some preachers will make statements like, "Come to Jesus and He will solve all your problems." When I surrendered to Christ, that's when my problems began!

So, sin is in our lives whether we like it or not, even if we are a Christian. The apostle Paul made it very clear that when you become a follower of Jesus you will still have that internal struggle, even if you've been a Christian for many years.

Five losses

Let's explore what we actually lost in the Garden of Eden when Adam and Eve first sinned. Look at the following five losses. The Gospel we preach is the only solution to these five things in society today.

We lost our personal relationship with God
After sin came into the world man no longer had a personal relationship with God. As a result, man could only commune with God via a third party. Throughout the Old Testament we are reminded of this fact and we see it vividly portrayed by the Old Testament sacrifices and rituals that had to take place. People could only come to God through the High Priest. Once a year, when the priest would go into the Holy of Holies with the sacrifice, the people would wait for

the sound of the bells ringing on the hem of his garment to know whether he was still alive or had been struck dead! If they could hear the bells ringing then they would know the sacrifice had been accepted and their sins were atoned for. This could only happen once a year. You and I, the common people, could never enter into the Holy of Holies. The High Priest was the only person allowed to do so.

This day was known as the "Day of Atonement" and in the Jewish calendar is called Yom Kippur. The Bible records the account in Leviticus chapter 16 when the High Priest would sacrifice two goats. One would be sacrificed and its blood would be taken into the Holy of Holies. The other was called the "scapegoat". After the priest had offered the first sacrifice he would come out of the Holy of Holies, confess the sins of the people over the head of the scapegoat, and then release it into the wilderness. This was symbolic of the people's sins being "taken away". This was echoed in the New Testament when John baptized Jesus, making the profound statement,

"Behold, the lamb of God who **takes away** the sin of the world."

The first goat was sacrificed to deal with the penalty of sin (propitiation) while the second goat was sacrificed for the presence of sin to be removed (expiation).

Sin separated man from God, yet He made a way possible for all through the death of His son Jesus Christ. Today, if you're not a Christian, then your sin is the barrier that is separating you from God. But there is good news: Jesus Christ came into this world to act as our High Priest. He died on a cross and shed His blood, once and for all, so that the relationship between man and God can be restored. We need to preach this Gospel like we've never preached it before!

The relationship between men and women

After sin came into the world a part of the "curse" that fell upon man was that man would rule over woman, when this had not been the situation before the fall.

> *"Your desire shall be for your husband, and he shall rule over you."*
>
> (Genesis 3:16)

When Jesus came and died on the cross, He came to restore this relationship. Now, in Christ, there is no longer a difference between man and woman. The bonds are free and we're all one in Jesus Christ.

> *"...there is neither male nor female; for you are all one in Christ Jesus."*
>
> (Galatians 3:28)

It affected business

If you're involved in business you will know that many people have absolutely no idea about what's going on any more. I write this at the height of an economic crisis in the UK. People's pension funds are not making what they hoped, businesses are going under, redundancies are commonplace. All of a sudden, things that we thought were secure are no longer safe. We want to blame everything and everyone else – international currency fluctuations, the price of oil, political turmoil, the cost of funding a war, but the reality is that it's the consequence of sin.

When sin came into the world look what happened: the ground ceased to yield bountiful fruit and man had to toil with the sweat of his brow. Every time you see a weed in the garden you are reminded of sin (if you haven't seen any weeds lately, it's only because you haven't been in the garden!). Weeds are always there; I guarantee it.

Business was affected because of sin and business is still affected today because of sin. People strive to overcome and counteract failing business with corruption and, more often than not, leadership and government are often to be found involved in this as well. The truth is, all that will restore thriving, profitable business in the land is the eradication of sin by the power of the Gospel.

It affected government

God gave Adam the job of ruling over this world, but He also gave him *worth* before He gave him *work*. A very common problem today is that a person's worth comes out of their work. The first question you often ask a new acquaintance is to find out what job they do. If they are unemployed, then suddenly they're relegated to the bottom of the social pile. On the other hand, if they've earned a PhD they're quite often considered to be much more important than others. We attribute worth to people according to their work, but this goes against the biblical grain.

God didn't do this to people. He gave worth before He gave work. He said,

"Let's make man in My own image ..."

Our worth, then, should come from knowing we've been made in the image of God. When God had given man worth He then gave him a job:

"Then the LORD God took the man and put him in the garden of Eden to tend and keep it"
(Genesis 2:15)

However, because of sin Adam ended up trying to rule over a world that was in rebellion.

It affected education
Education was also affected by the entrance of sin into the world. The Bible tells us that every day God came down into the Garden and spoke with Adam, giving him instructions and telling him what to do.

> *"And the* LORD *God commanded the man, saying, 'Of every tree of the garden you may freely eat; but of the tree of the knowledge of good and evil you shall not eat, for in the day that you eat of it you shall surely die.'"*
> (Genesis 2:16-17)

God took the trouble to educate man on this and no doubt many other aspects of life and governing the earth, but this education vanished along with the personal relationship between man and God.

That which was lost

This is why, like never before, we've got to preach the Gospel. We've got to show people the consequences of sin. Most people want to know whether there is life *before* death, never mind whether there is life *after* death. They are busy trying to discover whether there is any purpose to life now – and if so, what it is and what that means to them. Why are they on this planet? What are they supposed to do? There is only one answer to both those questions and the answer is a Person: Jesus Christ. You and I have the privilege and responsibility of telling others about Jesus, maybe today or maybe this week.

It says in Luke's gospel that the Son of Man came to seek and to save *that* which was lost. In other words, Jesus came to redeem every single thing that was affected by the fall – all of those things that we have just mentioned as being lost. He can put them back together better than they ever were. He came to redeem and to save *that* which was lost. The Gospel of Jesus Christ can therefore affect education, business, government, personal relationships and, most of all, it can affect your relationship with God the Father Himself. What a fantastic Gospel we preach!

Currently, I have the privilege of leading a ministry called Victory Outreach UK, that is committed to rehabilitating people who are in bondage to addiction of various kinds or who have found themselves drawn into a life of crime and have spent time in prison. I could fill pages and pages with the testimonies of those whose lives have been changed by this incredible Gospel. Here are just a couple. Their names have been changed to protect their identities.

> "My name is Kelli. I came to Victory outreach UK after a 15 year drug habit. I had tried everything to try and overcome my addiction and my way of life. I was stealing and committing crime daily, and had years and years of prison sentences, but nothing could release me from this bondage. Then I met Jesus and He has set me free and released me from Satan's grip."

> "Hiya, my name is Abi and I am 18 years old. God has completely transformed my life. Before coming to Victory Outreach UK my life was going from bad to worse and I knew that something had to change. I praise and thank Him so much for everything He's doing in my life. I give him all the glory! Amen!"

"Hi, my name is Angie. I was a heroin and crack addict for 19 years. I have committed crime and been in prison 28 times. Now, I've got a chance to change my life by walking with Jesus every day."

The list of changed lives could go on and on, but for many this Gospel is the best kept secret in the world.

> **"A lot of people who go to church *resemble* Christians, but they lack real authenticity. They have no living, vital relationship with Jesus Christ."**

All these Christians who carry their big black books and go into large buildings (most of the world doesn't even know what goes on inside these buildings!) – what are they achieving? They come, attend the service and go away to do their own thing until they come back again the following Sunday. In between their life is a poor example of biblical Christianity. There's got to be more we can share about being a Christian than this. In fact, there is a *lot more* to being a Christian. Jesus said,

"I have come that they may have life, and that they may have it more abundantly"

(John 10:10)

The foundation of character

A lot of people who go to church *resemble* Christians, but they lack real authenticity. They have no living, vital relationship with Jesus Christ. But Jesus, in the parable of the wheat and the tares (Matthew 13:24-30), warned that focusing our attention on removing the "tares" or unauthentic Christians in the Church, might damage authentic Christians.

The starting point of being an authentic Christian is being able to trust in God and becoming a trustworthy follower of Jesus. Why trust? Because unless we trust in God and trust that He has our best interests at heart, then we will hold Him at arm's length, not allowing Him to bring about a work of transformation in our lives. If that is the case then we will be living a poor imitation of biblical Christianity.

Many people who profess to be Christians are great worriers, and this belies their lack of trust in God. As we grow in relationship with Christ, we learn how to trust God. We learn how to commit things to Him in prayer and we find He is faithful to respond to our prayers. As we deepen in this relationship, God is able to gently and progressively transform us from the inside out by the power of His Holy Spirit working in us.

But trust is not always easy. It is like the story of the man who pushed a wheelbarrow across a tight wire stretched over Niagara Falls. It was one thing for observers to say they believed he could pull off this amazing stunt. But it was a different matter when he asked one of the observers to demonstrate their trust in his ability by climbing into the wheelbarrow! Really trusting God means climbing into the wheelbarrow.

When people first come to Christ, often their relationship with God is so fresh and vital that they find it easier to trust Him. Sadly, over time, our human tendency to complicate things and to say, "It can't be that easy – there must be more to it than that," soils the purity and simplicity of that trust. Instead of allowing our trust in God to diminish over time, we need to nurture it, so that we develop a true, meaningful and deep relationship with God that grows ever stronger as we allow the Holy Spirit to play His role in our lives.

> **"Authentic Christians are transparent.
> What you see is what you get with them."**

Solomon said,

> *"Trust in the Lord with all thine heart; and lean not unto thine own understanding. In all thy ways acknowledge him, and he shall direct thy paths."*
>
> (Proverbs 3:5-6, KJV)

There is the part we have to play: we trust in the Lord; and there is the part He plays: He directs our path. This is the starting point for authentic Christianity. The authentic Christian not only trusts God, but he is someone who is worthy of the trust of God's people.

Authentic Christians are transparent

If you have been in the Church very long, you will know there are people who are transparent, people who are evasive and others who are downright deceptive. And there are those who are in denial; they have issues in their lives and their relationships that they never acknowledge or deal with. These are the kinds of people who often are the source of division and confusion in the Church.

Authentic Christians are transparent. What you see is what you get with them. They have learned through hard experience that the transparent life is more likely to bring them the joy and peace of the Kingdom, so they are honest about what is happening in their own lives and they are honest about issues they have with other people.

Transparent people learn the wisdom of living according to John's plea that we be transparent in our relationship with God, with ourselves, and with other people (1 John 1:7-9).

That is, we live in confession of our sins, we find forgiveness for our sins, and we walk in truth and light with God and with others.

If it's true that many believers live out a pale version of the vibrant faith that characterized the lives of early believers, and I believe that it is, why is this? In Matthew chapter seven we read this salutary warning given by Jesus Himself:

> *"Not everyone who says to Me, 'Lord, Lord,' shall enter the kingdom of heaven, but he who does the will of My Father in heaven. Many will say to Me in that day, 'Lord, Lord, have we not prophesied in Your name, cast out demons in Your name, and done many wonders in Your name?' And then I will declare to them, 'I never knew you; depart from Me, you who practice lawlessness!'*
>
> (Matthew 7:21-23)

The NIV translation for verse 23 says,

> *"Then I will tell them plainly, 'I never knew you. Away from me, you evildoers!'"*

Note that in this particular verse Jesus isn't attacking the spirituality of the believers. He's not questioning their ability to prophesy, to speak in tongues or to cast out demons. Neither is He questioning their supernatural, spiritual ability. Instead, in this particular verse He says that it's those who practice "lawlessness" who will not inherit the kingdom of God. Or, put another way, those who do not do the "will of my Father". It's plain to see from this that the reason some people live Christian lives that don't achieve very much is not an issue of belief but behaviour. It is a *doing* issue, not a *thinking* issue.

Character is the measure by which Jesus looks at us and sees how spiritual we are. He doesn't look at our lives or the way we live our lives and give us the "all clear" to carry on behaving as we do. Morally, there are always going to be areas in our lives that are not in correct alignment with God's Word and these are contrary to the way we should live as Christians. Yet we come to church, call ourselves Christians and behave in a spiritual manner. This behaviour doesn't give a true picture of how spiritual we. Only our character determines this.

I see character as a product of an individual's moral qualities. It includes a variety of attributes, such as the existence or lack of integrity, courage, fortitude, honesty or loyalty. It also incorporates habitual sins or even non-habitual sins. The psychologist Lawrence Pervin defines moral character as "a disposition to behave expressing itself in consistent patterns of functioning across a range of situations."

As Christians our moral character is vitally important. We will not be judged by our spirituality but we will be judged according to our moral character, just as we read in the Bible. When we stand before Christ as our Judge and Saviour (and we all will one day) we will be judged by our moral character. It's so important to understand that our behaviour is affected by a true manifestation of our spiritual condition. This means that we can't just call ourselves Christians if we don't live like Christians. It also means that we cannot jump on our moral high horses to judge others because in doing this we would display a *lack* of moral character. Even if we are in a place where morally we have good values, we do not have the right to judge others. Rather, a spiritual and morally correct Christian will approach a person who is struggling, pick them up and help them on their way, whilst never pointing the finger. This was the example that Jesus set for us in His own behaviour.

The issue in this Scripture is that there's this internal struggle in each of us because of the Adamic nature we inherited. We know that before our new nature we just lived according to our own fleshly desires and had no conscience about doing what was wrong or doing things that were immoral. We had no conscience about them because we did not have the new nature living within us.

I want to give you a personal example of this. Before I became a Christian and a follower of Jesus Christ I did whatever I wanted and had no conscience that what I was doing was wrong. I did it, enjoyed it, loved it, partied, slept around, took as many drugs as I could and was never once kept awake at night by my conscience telling me I was doing wrong. I seemed to have no conscience at all.

However, most people do feel pangs of conscience over their life because the Bible says that God has placed "eternity in the hearts of all men". There is a side of us that has an eternal perspective and makes us question right and wrong. Back in my day, if we were ever interviewed by the Police they always used to ask the question, "Do you know the difference between right and wrong?" They did this because they wanted to know that we were clear in our conscience about the difference between right and wrong and the crimes we had committed before they conducted an interview.

> **"The constant application of biblical truth in our lives is the first step towards real, authentic Christianity that lives up to its name."**

Now, here's a dilemma: many people call themselves a Christian and yet are struggling with sin in their life. They tells themselves, surely I shouldn't have this sin in my life.

How does one deal with this? Firstly, it is important to know that this is the struggle that every believer has – the internal struggle mentioned earlier. The Apostle Paul wrestled with this issue just like every believer does. In Romans 7:19 NIV the apostle Paul is trying to express this in different ways. He says,

"For what I do is not the good I want to do; no, the evil I do not want to do—this I keep on doing."

Here is one of the greatest New Testament characters telling us that he struggled to understand the internal conflict between the new nature and the old nature; the good that he really wanted to do – the new nature wanting to do the Father's will – but finding within himself a strong desire and a strong bias and pull to do that which he despised. He would look at himself with eyes of condemnation and even condemn the things he himself would be thinking or considering or even doing.

How did Paul overcome this struggle? Firstly, we have to realise that the struggle remains within us to some extent until the day we die. After we have been a believer for many years, sin should not dominate our lives in the way it once did, but it is inevitable that we will still commit sin one way or another. The way in which Paul countered the onslaught of the fallen nature was by persistently applying the Word of God. The Bible is our basic tool for developing our character and so escaping the lure of sin and its downward drag. The more we apply the truth of the Word to our life, the more it will transform us as it gives us greater insight into the nature of Christ and the new nature we have received through the sacrifice of Jesus.

Paul taught that we must,

> "Be transformed by the renewing of your mind. Then you will be able to test and approve what God's will is – his good, pleasing and perfect will."
>
> (Romans 12:2)

The constant application of biblical truth in our lives is the first step towards real, authentic Christianity that lives up to its name.

CHAPTER 2

Choices

We've already seen that every one of us who makes the claim of being an authentic Christian lives with two natures. We have the old nature and we have the new nature. Now here's the reality: we therefore have the *choice* to live according to either. We can choose to live by the persuasion and the leading of the new nature or by the persuasion and the leading of the old nature. Here's where it gets difficult.

> **"The struggle most of us face is not with the devil; it's with ourselves.**
> **You are your biggest problem.**
> **I am my biggest problem!"**

If as a Christian you're living your life being dictated to by the old nature, you will bring spiritual depression to your new nature and as a result, you will feel unworthy, unclean and possibly even unsaved. You may believe that God doesn't love you any more because you can't live up to the standards of righteousness, the bar that He has set in the Bible.

Allow me to let you into a secret: no one on earth can live up to the bar that He has set. It's impossible! We need to see the conflict correctly. This is why the Bible says we must not be ignorant of sin's devices. Many of Paul's epistles to the Church, Romans, Galatians and other letters, addressed this conflict – the clash of the new nature versus the old nature. Paul was trying to get the Church to understand that often we don't need to be attacked by the devil in order to be ineffective – we have enough trouble just dealing with the problems of our own flesh!

And remember, the devil can only be in one place at one time. He is localised, a fallen angel. People often have this idea of God and the devil fighting each other, but they are not equal. The devil is down here! God is Sovereign King of all and the devil is under Him. The devil can be in one place at one time and there are only a limited amount of demons – they don't procreate. The Bible says that a third of them were cast out of heaven, which means they're limited and they can't be everywhere at once. But God is everywhere at once. He's omnipresent and He knows everything. Let's not give the devil credit where it's not due. He doesn't know everything.

However, the struggle most of us face is not with the devil; it's with ourselves. You are your biggest problem. I am my biggest problem! I get in my way all the time and you get in your own way. We often prevent ourselves from doing the things we long to do for God, things that we really want to do. We constantly hinder ourselves. Recognising this is one of the most helpful things you will ever do for yourself as a believer. If you make triumphalistic statements like, "I don't have any problems because I am reigning in Christ. I've overcome it all. There's no sin in my life," then you are walking around with spiritual blinkers on. The Bible says simply,

> *"If we say that we have no sin, we deceive ourselves, and the truth is not in us."*
>
> (1 John 1:8)

John the apostle was speaking to believers here – not non-Christians – saying that if we profess to have no sin we have deceived ourselves. To put it bluntly, if we don't admit to our sin, we are liars.

All of us are sinners in need of a saviour; every *one* of us, irrespective of how religious we are, how good we are and how nice and Christian we look. We all need a saviour and we all need to repent. Repentance is not a one-off occurrence, but an ongoing need and discipline that we have to develop. Authentic repentance leads to authentic forgiveness.

It is definitely the sin nature that's in view when John is talking about the sin in us. Furthermore, the entire passage is addressed to believers and includes *all* believers. John is strongly affirming that every born again person has a sin nature. It's very important we understand this because some Bible teachers will say we no longer have the sin nature once we have come to Christ, and that through baptism it's over, done and gone. But this is not true in my experience, nor the experience of 100% of the people I have counselled as a pastor.

However, we shouldn't build on experientialism, we should build on Scripture, so what does the Bible have to say about this? Romans 7 and Galatians 5 give us clear indications that we are constantly struggling with the old nature, the sinful nature that still resides within us.

"But now, it is no longer I who do it, but sin that dwells in me. For I know that in me (that is, in my flesh) nothing good dwells;"
(Romans 7:17-18)

"I say then: Walk in the Spirit, and you shall not fulfil the lust of the flesh. For the flesh lusts against the Spirit, and the Spirit against the flesh; and these are contrary

to one another, so that you do not do the things that you wish."

(Galatians 5:16-17)

The fact is, we are saved, we are *being* saved and we *will be* saved. That is to say, salvation has come to us, our souls have been cleansed and our names are written in the Lamb's Book of life. We're Christians and we love the Lord and our hearts are for Him, not against Him. We're know we're going to heaven when we die.

Here is the problem though: we're still here on earth dealing with the sinful nature that's within us. We have been forgiven, God is not going to judge us and spiritually our souls have been saved. When we die we will go to heaven to a spiritual eternity with Him and our physical bodies will die because of sin. Our bodies are no good this side of eternity because they're damaged goods. We can dress up and look pretty but we're damaged goods, all of us.

The flesh and the mind are interlinked all the time. When Paul speaks of the mind he's speaking of the flesh and when he speaks of the flesh, he's speaking of the mind. So our flesh, not just the physical, but also our minds where carnality resides, are damaged. Hence we think wrong and we do wrong. This is the sinful nature. When we receive Christ this sinful nature doesn't disappear.

Identifying the struggle

The reason why some of us struggle morally is because we have not fully identified where the struggle takes place. It is mostly between us and our sinful nature, not between us and the devil. Some evangelicals have taught, wrongly, that our struggles are due to our old nature being controlled by Satan. But when Christ died on the cross He broke the power of Satan in our lives. We have the *sinful* nature, not the devil in us. Satan does have control in the life of a non-Christian and holds full sway in their lives. They may put up a fight and try all kinds of things but he'll have them in his grip. However, when Jesus Christ moves into the heart and takes control there is a new tenant in the house. The power of Satan is broken. But the power of our own flesh remains. The old fleshly nature doesn't appreciate being pushed aside so he puts up a fight.

Once you receive the nature of Christ within you the old nature wants you to believe that it won't bring satisfaction and won't fulfil you, that it's only temporary. But God can give you eternal satisfaction and joy like you've never known. Happiness then is not based on what happens to us in life, but on obedience to God. The deepest desire of every believer is to love God with all their heart, soul and mind, and to love their neighbours as themselves. Deep down this is in all believers.

Here's the deal: if you screw up, as long as you have that deep down desire – as Wesley said, this grace that works within us – then God looks at the motive of the heart. That's why God could say of David, an adulterer,

> *"I have found David the son of Jesse, a man after My own heart"*
>
> (Acts 13:22)

How could God say this? Deep down David's new nature – God working within him – was desiring and longing to serve God with all of his heart, even though he gave in to his old nature.

So we have this conflict in our lives and we have a choice to make. Some people evade this issue by denying that a genuine believer will experience struggles. They declare that either initial salvation or the baptism of the Spirit (the second blessing) destroys the capacity for sin. This is not true. It's exactly what John was warning against when he said if we think we have no sin we deceive ourselves.

Crucify the flesh

Some people make the mistake of trying to suppress the old nature by observing certain rules. The problem is that it's done in their own strength, with their own flesh, the very thing they're trying to get delivered from. Eventually they can't sustain this and fail, which is why some people will respond to altar call after altar call. It is all about self effort and it doesn't work.

Paul said,

> *"I crucify the flesh daily,"*

and

> *"those who are Christ's have crucified the flesh with its passions and desires"*
>
> (Galatians 5:24)

He reveals that the only way to master our old nature with its desires is to come to Christ in constant surrender– on a daily basis, in fact.

The error of self-effort becomes all the more apparent when you are married. I have been married for ten years, so I'm a novice compared to some, but here is what I have discovered: if individually we suffer from "dualism" – the battle between our new and old natures – then when we are married this becomes "quadrupalism", because we are now in an intimate relationship with another person who is experiencing the same struggles! When you marry you become "one" and you begin to discover your spouse's old nature and they begins to discover yours, and it's not nice! Married couples, therefore, need to come together in agreement and battle for the moral ground, standing together when sin tries to come into their marriage. We need to apply scriptural reasoning in every situation so that the enemy will not get any foothold in the marriage. This is why people end up getting divorced. They allow the sinful nature in their marriage to be the dominating factor and they don't deal with it. In fact they ignore it, live with it and somehow justify it.

But in marriage, as in our personal lives, this is true: if you don't kill your sin, your sin will kill you. If you don't stop it then you are allowing the sinful nature, and if you allow it in your home and in your family eventually it will spread to your kids. We cannot "manage" the flesh, we have to choose to kill it. This is known as the doctrine of Mortification. Paul said it like this:

"For if you live according to the flesh you will die; but if by the Spirit you put to death the deeds of the body, you will live."

(Romans 8:13)

Mortification is killing off the deeds of the body and choosing to say, "I am not going to do that, I choose not to, because the conscience of my nature says that is not right."

"People make countless excuses to justify why they are the way they are ... the truth is, there is always a deeper, internal reason."

Who's responsible?

A characteristic of the sinful nature is that it never accepts blame. It always shifts blame. When confronted with the fact that he has sinned, Adam immediately said,

> *"The woman whom You gave to be with me, she gave me of the tree, and I ate."*
>
> (Genesis 3:12)

Eve's excuse was,

> *"The serpent deceived me, and I ate"*
>
> (Genesis 3:13)

People make countless excuses to justify why they are the way they are. They say, "It's the church's fault. That's why I drifted away from God." The truth is, there is always a deeper, internal reason. No church is perfect, but even if a person had a bad experience at a church, that is no reason to turn away from God. We are responsible for the choices that we make in our lives. I am responsible for every single choice. Good, bad or indifferent, I am responsible. My character will always determine my choices, which is why moral character is so very important. If I'm living my life in the new nature of Christ, this character will determine my choices. But if I live under the old nature, I will make the wrong choices every time. We've all done it. How do we overcome this conflict?

"It's the devil's fault ..."

Many Christians will blame Satan for everything. When anything bad happens, the blame tends to be directed towards him. Whilst there is a sense in which that is true, many people use it as a "get out clause" to avoid dealing with their own character issues. Such a view fails to take into consideration all the other issues like our personal responsibility for our own actions. It's too easy for us to blame the devil and excuse ourselves. I have heard too many Christians say, in effect, "The devil made me do it."

People are inclined to blame the devil in order to remove their guilt, justify their actions, and ignore their responsibility and the things God wants to teach them through their suffering. This has been true from the very beginning, as we see so clearly in Eve's answer to God in explanation of why she sinned. She immediately blamed the serpent when faced with her sin in the garden. Adam too had his scapegoat, blaming Eve and even the Lord Himself:

"The woman made me do it, the one you gave me."

Certainly, as the deceiver and liar, Satan instigated the temptation, but Eve responded with negative volition, unbelief, and disobedience, and Adam failed to stay true to his responsibility as the leader in his family.

"Our primary focus needs to be not on Satan, but on the Lord and our responsibility to grow in Christ."

Today, regardless of the various external sources of temptation (Satan and the world), the final source is our own sinful nature or the lusts and self-centered desires of our own hearts. But in Christ, by virtue of the finished work and victory of the Savior, we are victors; He has provided everything we need to defeat sin and Satan (1 John 4:4; 5:4-5, Romans 6:1-14).

However, having said all this, it is equally true that through the world system and the demonic hosts that Satan controls we are constantly faced with the power and activity of Satan in more ways than we can possibly imagine. As Paul warns, our battle is not only with flesh and blood, but with supernatural powers that are constantly in operation in the sons of disobedience and against the body of Christ (Ephesians 2:1-3; Ephesians 6:10-13).

When Satan can attack us he will, and only God knows how much of what we face is the direct result of the devil's onslaughts. At the same time, much of our suffering is the direct result of our own self-induced misery, sometimes as a product of our ignorance, or unbelief, or indifference, or a combination of all of the above. So Scripture tells us to resist the devil and he will flee from us, to put on the whole armour of God, to be controlled by means of the Spirit, to have Word-filled lives, to walk circumspectly and in wisdom, and to be on alert because of the activity of Satan who is constantly on the prowl.

But there are two things we should not assume:

1. That everything evil that happens to us is the result of direct Satanic attack. Though he is indirectly involved, some of what happens is simply the result of life in a fallen world.

2. We should not assume that all our suffering is the product of our own sin or indifference to the Lord. Job was a righteous man who walked with God, yet for His own purposes and for Job's spiritual growth (all testing is ultimately designed for our growth), God allowed Satan to attack him. Paul too was a godly, spirit-filled man, yet he experienced a thorn in the flesh which he defined as a messenger of Satan. It was an affliction God used as a

tool in Paul's life to teach him some important spiritual lessons (2 Corinthians 12).

The Lord healed all kinds of illness, but a careful study of the New Testament shows us that only a small portion of these illnesses were actually attributed to Satan or demonic causes. The same can be said of the writings of the Apostle Paul. He spoke of Trophimus who was sick, but he never suggested this was the product of direct Satanic attack. Timothy may have been experiencing some kind of stomach difficulty, but Paul's advice was simply to take a little wine for his problem. No mention of Satan or demons.

A general reading of the epistles puts the emphasis not on the demonic, but on our own responsibility to appropriate our assets in Christ. So while we need to acknowledge Satan's constant activity and be alert, our primary focus needs to be not on Satan but on the Lord and our responsibility to grow in Christ. It is often a cop-out, pure and simple, for us to blame the devil when what is needed is honest to God personal examination and confession that we might be restored to fellowship, learn the spiritual lessons needed, and be made like Him as a part of the process of growth and maturity in Christ.

We need to deal with our sin and heed Paul's advice. Paul says,

"Likewise you also, reckon yourselves to be dead indeed to sin, but alive to God in Christ Jesus our Lord."
(Romans 6:11)

Later in Romans he writes,

"There is therefore now no condemnation to those who are in Christ Jesus, who do not walk according to the

> *flesh, but according to the Spirit. For the law of the Spirit of life in Christ Jesus has made me free from the law of sin and death. For what the law could not do in that it was weak through the flesh, God did by sending His own Son in the likeness of sinful flesh, on account of sin: He condemned sin in the flesh, that the righteous requirement of the law might be fulfilled in us who do not walk according to the flesh but according to the Spirit."*
>
> (Romans 8:1-4)

We overcome the flesh by walking in the Spirit. Whichever nature we feed will become the predominant feature in our life, so we need to feed the nature that we want to be the most powerful, so that it will be instrumental in determining our choices.

How do we feed our new nature and walk in the Spirit? By reading scriptures, listening to the ministry of others, spending time with God, worshipping, praying and talking to Jesus. I am constantly amazed at how many people don't talk to Jesus, thinking it's some kind of weird and wacky thing. Jesus hears you and wants a relationship with you. He'll talk with you and walk with you. Read His Word and He'll speak to you. This is feeding your spiritual man. The classic book by Watchman Nee called *The Spiritual Man* deals thoroughly with this issue and I would recommend it to anyone. It talks about the need to feed the inward, the spiritual man, to build ourselves up by praying in the Holy Spirit. It's all about prayer, sanctifying oneself, praying and studying the Scriptures. These are the things that will give strength and power to the new nature.

Unpardonable sin

Hebrews chapter 10 deals with an issue that has become known as the "unpardonable sin". I mention it here because I find that many Christians get confused about it and live under guilt, thinking that they have somehow angered God.

"For if we sin wilfully after we have received the knowledge of the truth, there no longer remains a sacrifice for sins, but a certain fearful expectation of judgment, and fiery indignation which will devour the adversaries. Anyone who has rejected Moses' law dies without mercy on the testimony of two or three witnesses. Of how much worse punishment, do you suppose, will he be thought worthy who has trampled the Son of God underfoot, counted the blood of the covenant by which he was sanctified a common thing, and insulted the Spirit of grace?"

(Hebrews 10:26-29)

Many Bible scholars, especially some of the early reformists such as Calvin and Berkhof, have taken these scriptures (which basically say that if we sin wilfully we're condemned) and include them into the context of Jesus' comments in Matthew chapter 12, where He said,

"Therefore I say to you, every sin and blasphemy will be forgiven men, but the blasphemy against the Spirit will not be forgiven men. Anyone who speaks a word against the Son of Man, it will be forgiven him; but whoever speaks against the Holy Spirit, it will not be forgiven him, either in this age or in the age to come."

(Matthew 12:31-32)

To clarify, Hebrews 10 is speaking about people who many scholars consider to be apostates. In other words, they have not just disbelieved, but they have deliberately turned their backs on God, denied sacred things and ridiculed them. They've decided, for whatever reason, to literally spit in God's face and walk away. Also, they have no consciousness of their sin any more and don't feel what they're doing is wrong. Having once received the knowledge of truth, these are people who trample underfoot the Blood and the Covenant, who insult the Spirit of grace.

This is not the same thing that Jesus was referring to, but many believers read this and worry about having offended the Holy Spirit and they condemn themselves simply because they still have a sinful nature. They come to church and worship Jesus, yet they return home and know they're not holy. Well, the fact is you are not as holy as you sing you are and I'm not as holy as much as I sing I am or pray that I am! It's all because we have the sinful nature. But we are not in that category where we are totally rejected, cut off or cast away.

Louis Berkhof says about this particular Scripture:

"In those who have committed this sin we may therefore expect to find pronounced hatred for God, a defiant attitude to Him and all that is divine, delight in ridiculing and slandering that which is holy, and absolute unconcern respecting the welfare of their soul and the future life."

Berkhof takes this verse and explains that those who've committed this sin, the unpardonable sin, will have those attributes. Here's what he says of those who have not committed this sin:

"In view of that fact that this sin is not followed by repentance, we may be reasonably sure that they who fear that they have committed it, who worry about it, and who desire the prayers of others for them, have not committed it."

Dr Henry M. Morris says, "The unforgivable sin of speaking against the Holy Spirit has been interpreted in various ways, but the true meaning cannot contradict other Scripture. It is unequivocally clear that the one unforgivable sin is permanently rejecting Christ. Thus, speaking against the Holy Spirit is equivalent to rejecting Christ with such finality that no future repentance is possible. 'My spirit shall not always strive with man'. ... In the context of this particular passage (Matthew 12:22-32), Jesus had performed a great miracle of creation, involving both healing and casting out a demon, but the Pharisees rejected this clear witness of the Holy Spirit. Instead they attributed His powers to Satan, thus demonstrating an attitude permanently resistant to the Spirit, and to the deity and saving Gospel of Christ."[1]

If you are living with the sin nature and crucifying it every day, but still deep down inside of you there is a longing and desire to be free to do what Christ wants you to do, to live like Christ and think like Him, then you are not in this category. It's important to teach this because a lot of Christians condemn themselves and walk away from God because they take the sinful nature as a dominating factor and wonder, "How can I call myself a Christian when I still struggle with this?" But you will struggle until they put you in the ground! You won't get to a place where you're completely free of sin and temptation. You'll never get there.

---

[1] Henry M. Morris, The Defender's Study Bible (Iowa Falls, Iowa: World Bible Publishers, 1995)

The Apostle Paul talked of this constantly, which is why he says we cannot master the flesh or manage it, all we can do is to "kill the flesh every day", to make a conscious decision to live right.

> **"It doesn't matter how sinful you are; God loves you. He wants to forgive you and cleanse you, to give you His new nature."**

But if we do sin we have an advocate with the Father. If we confess our sins He is faithful and just to forgive us and to cleanse us from all sin. So God says to us, "I love you so much. I know that you're struggling right now with the sinful nature and it's not until I come and give you a new body at the resurrection that you will be free. Until then you will continue to struggle, but allow my Spirit to work in you and nurture the new man, the inward man in you. Feed it, look after it and nurture it."

It's so refreshing to know that I'm not the only one struggling with sin or the temptation to sin. I'm not the only one and the same goes for you. Here's the good news: for those who've received the new nature of Christ we have a consciousness about it, which means we're aware of it. We don't like it, and that is because it offends and hurts the One who died for us. It's good to be aware of this because we therefore cannot stay in sin without repenting. We need to be continually living a life of repentance before the cross, coming to Him and saying, "Jesus, forgive me. I am a sinner."

It doesn't matter how sinful you are; God loves you. He wants to forgive you and cleanse you, to give you His new nature. Someone once said to me "Would you throw all this away and go back to the world?" There's no chance, no chance at all, was my reply. Then the person asked, "Even if you weren't preaching and you didn't have all the perks that come with being in ministry?" The answer is still no. The new nature would not allow me to. I couldn't. I've been back to South Wales, back to where the guys are smoking weed, fixing in flats and bed-sits. I've gone in there and had not one single desire or passion to do the same. None whatsoever. I was addicted to those things in the past. I loved to do them; they felt fantastic. But I have no desire or passion for them now because I have no love for them and we will always pursue what we have a love for, for whatever is in our heart.

Thank God that I have crucified the flesh in that area. Remember, if we don't kill our sin, our sin will kill us. Put to death the deeds of the body and live in the newness of life that Christ has come to give you.

Hallmarks of an Authentic Christian

CHAPTER 3

> "You have been bought with a price
> and you are not your own."

1 Corinthians 6:19 says,

> "...do you not know that your body is the temple of the Holy Spirit who is in you, whom you have from God, and you are not your own?"

According to Scripture we are the temple of the Holy Spirit and the Spirit lives inside of us. This is one crucial reason why there is no need for people to chase after an external "experience" of the Spirit. I don't know about you, but I certainly wouldn't want to receive from anywhere else other than God when it comes to my spiritual life. My number one source has to be Him.

> **"This first hallmark of a true, authentic Christian is that we understand we have been bought with a price and we are not our own. This is the great plan of salvation."**

As Christians we are responsible to God. The old fashioned teaching used to say, "I am your servant, Lord, and you are my Master." However, the consumer mentality of our society, which has so often permeated the Christian Church, has caused this way of thinking to be reversed and on many occasions we believe that we're the master and that God is our servant. Many Christians seem to think that God is there purely to answer their wishes like some kind of cosmic Genie and that they can blab it, grab it , name it, claim it, take it home and frame it – whatever "it" might be – just as long as they want it enough and pray continually for what they desire.

I believe that God wants us to stop talking and continually asking for what we want because His grace alone is sufficient for us and we need nothing more. If God never did another miracle in my life I would still serve Him with all of my heart because He loves me, He died for me and He doesn't need to do any more than that. Do you feel the same?

This first hallmark of a true, authentic Christian is that we understand we have been bought with a price and we are not our own. This is the great plan of salvation. Jesus came to purchase your soul. He did so because your soul was already destined for hell from birth, because of what we understand as original sin. But this gift of God, the person of Jesus Christ, came to the world to die on a cross to cleanse your soul so that your spirit could also be regenerated and made alive to God.

"For God so loved the world He gave His only begotten Son" (John 3:16), that you could be a forgiven, redeemed person. When you die you will leave this life and will go to heaven, not hell.

If we look at the life of Jesus we can see that He was a missionary. He didn't come to Earth just to perform miracles and they were certainly not in His ministry just to authenticate His deity. He said of himself, *"I am"*, speaking of Him being God, on several occasions. So He definitely did not need to perform miracles just to prove His deity. And although the people around Him may have needed to see to believe, Jesus said,

"Blessed are you who have not seen and believe"
(John 20:29)

The fact that we have been bought with a price brings us great responsibility. My life and your life are not our own. We are not owned by our employers or by our parents and definitely not by any particular church. We are the sheep of God's pasture. God has complete and absolute ownership of our life, so we are responsible to Him. He is our master and we are His servants!

The subtlety of the consumer Gospel has reversed our thinking here. Prosperity preaching has a lot to answer for in this respect, but I believe that message has changed over time and become so blatantly and obviously unscriptural that people are beginning to see through it. The new danger to authentic Christianity is the message that we should do away with material prosperity and instead pursue spiritual prosperity, which is disguised and clothed with so much deception. What I mean by this is people seeking only after spiritual experiences that do not lead to a change in character or result in any fruit.

Personally, I struggle to reconcile much of the manifestation of the Spirit shown on Christian television with an authentic move of God's Spirit. Does this mean God doesn't want us to have spiritual experiences? It doesn't, but we must always go back to the ultimate reference, God's Word, to test whether something is an authentic move of God.

Some people may challenge what I am saying here as being legalistic, but I don't believe it is. Being a man or a woman of the Bible isn't being legalistic and there is no doubt that you cannot go wrong by following God's Word. Heaven and earth will pass away, but His Word will never pass away. Spiritual eras and movements within the Christian Church will come and go, but His Word will never fail. God has sworn Himself by His Word He has made a covenant by His Word to keep it and to perform His Word. It is therefore crucial that everything is measured by Scripture.

I have sought to try and understand spiritual experiences in the Bible from the day of Pentecost right through the Acts of the Apostles and I find that all of Paul's letters are constantly addressing the same issues that concern me in the Church today. Paul told the believers at Corinth,

"You're a very spiritual people. You all want to prophesy and you all want to speak in tongues, but let me try and bring you some scriptural and biblical decency, which is glorifying to Christ, and not off the wall."

Most situations I have seen that claim to be moves of God do so for the same reason: because miracles are happening. This seems to be the only thing people need to give it validity. However, they don't question the theology or the doctrine that is being taught. All they say is that people are being healed, but I know people who've been to a faith healer and have been healed. I know people who have been to clairvoyants, have been told their future and the clairvoyant was right. Was that God? I like to ponder what my old pastor used to say: "If the devil can put sickness on, he can take it off." I don't say that to denigrate any genuine move of God, but we need to be careful. Remember we are not our own. Let's not be gullible Christians.

"Whoever desires to come after me, let him deny himself"

In Mark's Gospel Jesus makes a challenging statement to His followers:

> *"When He had called the people to Himself, with His disciples also, He said to them, 'Whoever desires to come after Me, let him deny himself, and take up his cross, and follow Me.'"*
>
> (Mark 8:34)

This scripture can be very hard to take for a number of reasons. For one, I like to enjoy my life and when I'm told I have to deny myself it can make me feel very sombre. However, it's not necessarily talking about denying ourselves things we enjoy such as watching football on television, shopping or socialising. What it's saying is this: we must deny anything that places itself above the *will* of God in our life.

Everything in our life from family, finances, relationships and jobs must be subservient to God's will. Jesus said in Matthew 7 that only those who do the will of His Father will inherit the kingdom. This doesn't mean those who just talk about the will of His Father, (because a lot of people do just talk about it), but it means only those who *do the will* of His Father will inherit the kingdom.

Knowing God's will and doing it is authentic Christianity. An authentic Christian isn't someone who just comes to church week in week out for years, sits in the pew, worships God and sings the songs. Think about it. Are you an authentic Christian? Do you truly believe that your life is not your own, that it has been bought with a price and that Jesus is your master and you are His servant? And do you place things above the will of God such as career, finances and relationships?

God doesn't say that you can't have any of these things, but they must be within the will of God for your life. It must always be the overriding factor. This is the mark of an authentic Christian. It's not somebody who does the opposite, when all they want is whatever they can get out of life, having all the pleasures and chasing materialism. If you look at the early Christians you will see in them a great amount of sacrificial living and humility. Ask yourself the question and be really honest with what you perceive and what you see in the Christian Church. Is what you're seeing sacrificial and full of humility?

I believe that the Christian Church has become a bit of a show in recent years. Those who shout the loudest, who are the most charismatic and the weirdest, often get all the publicity and press, and pull great crowds. What happened to denying yourself, taking up your cross and following Jesus? This is not a morbid Gospel message. It's the Gospel that Jesus Christ preached. He never preached, "Come to me and I'll make all things *well*." He said,

"Come to me and I'll make all things new."

There is a massive difference in these two statements.

"Knowing God's will and doing it is authentic Christianity."

Let's just think of Jesus for a moment. Imagine He's here. He starts doing miracles and so the television crews come into town and decide they want to film what He is doing. (I'm not too sure whether Jesus would have allowed it, but let's just suppose He did). So, Jesus starts doing all kinds of miracles, all kinds of wonderful things are happening and it draws bigger and bigger crowds. What would be the very reason for Jesus drawing crowds? Why would He want to draw crowds? There is only one reason: because He's a missionary. He came on a mission to seek and to save the lost and this was the only reason. Jesus would have drawn the crowds to Him for the sole purpose of salvation.

If we look at the Book of Acts we can find the reason for an outpouring of the Spirit. The main point of this outpouring was that many people were added to the Church daily:

"Then those who gladly received his word were baptized; and that day about three thousand souls were added to them."

(Acts 2:41)

So it makes me concerned that in modern day outpourings people who are responding to altar calls to be born again are already born again. People are being baptised when they've already been baptised, but because it's on television they want to be seen by others and get re-baptised in the name of the Father, the Son and Holy Ghost. This is so wrong!

Again, some may want to argue the point that in these situations miracles are happening. I believe it is dangerous to be so vulnerable and spiritually immature to think that just because miracles are happening it makes it an authentic move of God. Scripture warns us that many will come with false "anointings". We must not forget that Satan is powerful. He's an angel of light and he comes in many guises. If we look at cults around the world today, most of them claim to have been started when someone was visited by an "angel". For example, Joseph Smith claimed to have seen an angel who then showed him where plates were buried in the ground. He dug these up and from them we get the book of Mormon, thus the whole of the Mormon cultish religion. It's deception, just the same as Jehovah's Witnesses. I'm not attacking these people individually, but I am speaking doctrinally. Do not entertain them as what they believe is doctrinally wrong.

I believe that there's a counterfeit spirituality happening around the world and Christians need to be very careful to make sure they're not being deceived or seduced by the latest, greatest thing. Instead we need to learn the discipline of denying ourselves. We need to remind ourselves that we are owned by God. He provided our salvation and therefore we take on a life of sacrifice and service to Him. Sacrifice isn't often preached today because it doesn't fit in with our lifestyles since our world is mainly geared towards getting, getting and getting. But remember that it's not about you or me: it's about Jesus Christ and His will being worked through our lives and that is going to cost us because being a disciple is a sacrifice.

Some people think that coming to church twice on a Sunday is a "cost". This isn't cost. Cost is when people say all manner of things against you for His name's sake, when they wrongly accuse you and say things against you because you're standing up for Him. This is what sacrifice is. It's a young couple selling everything because the call of God is for them to go and work with AIDS victims in Africa. They sell everything, don't ask for a penny, jump on a plane and fly out there and nurse dying babies without one single television camera telling the world how wonderful they are. This is sacrifice.

Ask yourself, "What am I actually sacrificing?" An authentic Christian always has sacrifice in their life.

Walk in His teachings and practices

Sadly, many people think that they don't need to try and keep to the Scriptures in the sense of the Law and statutes of God, but actually Scripture teaches us that we should. We shouldn't just throw out the Old Testament because we think it's not relevant post Jesus dying on the cross, convincing ourselves that He cancelled it out. Jesus, against popular opinion, never came to abolish the Law, He came to fulfil the Law. So we have a responsibility to do the best we can, with the knowledge we have, to live like Christ lived. It's no good saying, "I'm a Christian but I can't keep the Ten Commandments, so I'll just break all of them." We have to do our best to keep what we can and let God deal with what we can't. That is living under grace.

A true disciple is someone who walks in God's ways. In the Book of Ezekiel God speaks about Israel and says,

"Listen, if you keep My statutes and you keep My ordinances; if you walk in My ways then you will live and you enter into the land of blessing and prosperity that I have prepared for you. But if you don't, you won't."

People get upset with God because as Christians they're waiting and nothing seems to happen. They're praying because they need this to happen, that to happen, and yet it doesn't. But they fail to see that they're not walking in the statutes and ordinances of God. It's an age-old word called obedience. We used to preach it in the old Church, of which we definitely need a revival.

Obedience and sacrifice: these are words that we've cast to one side because they don't fit in with the contemporary, modern way of doing church, especially in people's theology. But it's very theological. Jesus was obedient unto death, even death on the cross. This was obedience *and* sacrifice. I'll tell you why we struggle in churches to get volunteers: it's a lack of sacrifice and obedience.

I was blessed because when I was born again it was in a classical Pentecostal environment. Most of my roots are in Pentecostalism, not in sensationalism. I remember at the end of every service there were two calls: a call for salvation and a call to be a missionary. This happened in every service. As a result I've been a missionary to more countries than you can imagine because there was a desire in me that wanted to just do whatever God wanted me to do. When an appeal is given at the front of a church will you go? When God wants you to go will you give up all of your hopes and desires?

"Authentic Christianity is often to be found at the end of church newsletter, as a postscript to everything else: P.S. we are having a collection for the poor next Sunday."

We must be people with the hallmarks of true, authentic Christianity, those that live a life of obedience to Jesus Christ. Look at James 2. James is an elder of the church in Jerusalem and he is also one if the key apostles, the brother of Jesus. He is explaining to the Christian Church and to the council that there is a problem with those who claim to be Christians, but who are only interested in spirituality – they are not doing any of the things that Christians should do. These people, James says, say all the right things and sing all the songs, but the problem is in their works.

Scripture says that we are justified by faith in Christ alone, not by our works – otherwise we could claim to have had a hand in our salvation. But God will judge us when we die according to our works and the motives we had for doing them on the earth. In Heaven we will be rewarded according to the extent of our works on the earth. In other words, faith and works go together. It is unbalanced to have one without the other. James criticised the believers of his day for ignoring the needs of the poor. "If a poor man comes into the congregation and he needs food and clothes on his back and you say, 'Go away my brother, be blessed and be filled...'" then where is your faith? James wanted to know.

"But someone will say, 'You have faith, and I have works.' Show me your faith without your works, and I will show you my faith by my works."

(James 2:18)

Authentic Christianity is often to be found at the end of a church newsletter, as a postscript to everything else: P.S. we are having a collection for the poor next Sunday. So often we have our priorities completely confused! We get so engrossed in the spiritual aspects of our faith that we forget the practical. Notice what Jesus says about those He will judge:

"Many will say to Me in that day, 'Lord, Lord, have we not prophesied in Your name, cast out demons in Your name, and done many wonders in Your name?' And then I will declare to them, 'I never knew you; depart from Me, you who practice lawlessness!'"

(Matthew 7:22-23)

He won't be saying to people, "You fed the poor, you visited prisoners, I never knew you, depart from me." Instead, He is talking about spiritual gifts that have been exercised by Christians and yet He can still say, "I don't even know you."

A description of authentic Christianity is found in Matthew 25:

> "Then the King will say to those on His right hand, 'Come, you blessed of My Father, inherit the kingdom prepared for you from the foundation of the world: for I was hungry and you gave Me food; I was thirsty and you gave Me drink; I was a stranger and you took Me in; I was naked and you clothed Me; I was sick and you visited Me; I was in prison and you came to Me.'"
>
> (Matthew 25:34-36)

This is what we should believe and act out as the Christian Church. The Church will only get so far on spiritual gas. It will get a lot further on Christian living. A big problem for Jesus was that people always wanted to see the power and the miracles, yet Jesus did more acts of kindness than He did miracles in the Gospels. If you read carefully and look at what Jesus actually did and said to people, the compassion that He had for people and the way that He ministered to them, it is absolutely amazing!

Every miracle Jesus performed was carried out so that a need might be met, but He did not necessarily meet all of a person's needs. I find that some people leave the Church because they believed the lie, "Come to Jesus and everything will be fine. All your needs will be met ..." When that doesn't happen for them, then they leave. In this case the seed has indeed fallen by the wayside into a rocky place because that isn't what God says in His word. God didn't say He would deliver you from all your problems. But what He did say was this:

> "If you come to Me I will help you. Ask in My name, I will give you according to My will."

Take note though that it must be *"... according to My will."* His will for you might be that you need to struggle for a bit in order to learn some lessons! Maybe God is trying to teach you some things! It's like that with children. You don't always bail your kids out because sometimes you need them to experience certain things in order to teach them a valuable lesson.

Let's remember, then, the hallmarks of authentic Christianity. True believers are those who

◊ Know that they have been bought with a price and they belong to God.

◊ Deny themselves and are prepared to live a life of sacrifice.

◊ Walk in Christ's teaching and practices.

Allow yourself to be stamped with these hallmarks of authentic Christianity, just as a jeweller would mark a gem, allowing others to see Christ living within you.

Four Lies of Discouragement

CHAPTER 4

I want to look at four common misconceptions that often cause people to hold back in fulfilling their God-given purposes. I call these the four lies of discouragement.

Have you ever noticed that when you come to church and God really blesses and encourages you, something then happens when you go outside the door: your car won't start or somebody upsets you or you go home and the dinner's burnt? Anything can happen. The devil will always try to discourage us so let's make sure we are aware of these lies.

I'm not good enough to serve God

Under the Old Covenant, a person was disqualified from being a priest if he had certain physical defects. One of these was blindness, which I find interesting because there is a spiritual parallel for us – how can anyone serve the purposes of God in their life if they are spiritually blind? We need Jesus to open your eyes so we can see how much He loves us and cares about us.

In Leviticus the extent of these physical defects is spelled out:

> *"For any man who has a defect shall not approach: a man blind or lame, who has a marred face or any limb too long, a man who has a broken foot or broken hand, or is a hunchback or a dwarf, or a man who has a defect in his eye, or eczema or scab, or is a eunuch. No man of the descendants of Aaron the priest, who has a defect, shall come near to offer the offerings made by fire to the* LORD. *He has a defect; he shall not come near to offer the bread of his God."*
>
> (Leviticus 21:18-21)

Here we have a fascinating picture of the need for a perfect Christ to come and stand in the place of broken humanity. How many of us would be immediately disqualified from being priests in the Old Testament because of our physical defects? All of us have got something wrong! Aren't you glad that our High Priest came into this world to take flat-nosed, broken-footed, crooked-backed dwarves with disease from head to foot, and He washed us in His blood and qualified us to be kings and priests to our God? How amazing!

We don't get excited enough about what being a Christian really means. When you go to work on a Monday and people ask what you did at the weekend, too many of us say, "Oh, I *just* went to church…" We talk like this all the time. But we need to wake up and see the reality of what being an authentic Christian means. You are a priest and you've been called by God to serve this generation! We've got to start living that life.

Only a "minister" can be really used by God

The idea of "consumer church" has done much to fuel the idea that church is a show which is run from the front while people sit in the pews waiting to be entertained. But long before this, the divide between laity and clergy created the idea that you needed to be "ordained" and have special training and special knowledge to minister to others. That there is a difference between fulltime clergy and laity is a lie of the devil! God has blessed the Church with the Ephesians' gifts only to equip others to do the work of the ministry. Remember, it is not for them to do the work, but instead to equip *us* to do the work. So many Christians are passive when it come to their faith, but we can do better than this. We can see more people saved and we need to break this lie.

In many churches the pastors are mainly concerned with keeping the people in the pews happy. But church is not all about keeping people happy – it is all about pleasing Jesus! It's all about fulfilling our destiny and doing what God wants us to do. There is a sphere of influence which you have that your pastors will never have because they don't know the people you know. *You* are the best Christian that somebody knows! This could be a frightening thought, but it's true. Therefore we need to start living the sort of life that will help that person want to know more about Jesus Christ.

The Bible makes no distinction between clergy and laity under the New Covenant. We read,

*"But you are a chosen generation, a royal priesthood, a holy nation, His own special people, that **you** may proclaim the praises of Him who called you out of darkness into His marvellous light."*

(1 Peter 2:9-12)

In other words, in God's Kingdom there is a definite and specific job for you. The words of an old Gospel chorus say,

"There's a work for Jesus none but you can do."

We have to recognise the truth of these words. If we don't then we will put more and more pressure on our leaders and rely more heavily on those who minister the Word of God. But God has put these people in the church to equip us to do the job and to help us to get out there to where we have a sphere of influence, resulting in people being born again. We need to remember that we are a royal priesthood, agents acting on God's behalf to usher in His rule and reign.

The Bible says we are all kings and priests. You have been chosen by God to be a priest and to take Jesus Christ to the people. What a fantastic thing. The God-ordained ministers in your church who stand in the pulpit are there to provide you with the teaching so that you can do the work of the ministry and fulfil your role as a priest. So we can't come to church and just give them a mark out of ten every week: "That was 8 out of 10 ... not bad ... Could do better ... 7 out of 10 ..." etc. We must allow God to use our church leaders to equip us to fulfil our destiny as kings and priests in the name of Jesus Christ. That's why we are here. Don't not believe this lie of discouragement. If you have been born again then the Bible calls you a priest before God, so start living like one! Stop feeling sorry for yourself and start living like a priest. Jesus Christ died so that you and I could become priests, could become kings and could be a holy nation.

It is interesting to remember that before a priest could serve he had to wash himself. The blood of Jesus Christ washes us and cleanses us from all of our sin, preparing us to do the work of a priest. Outside of this we are filthy, dirty, rotten, stinking sinners – yet the blood of Jesus cleanses us. You are therefore qualified to be a priest because of the blood of Jesus. What an amazing thing.

I'll never be as effective as a fulltime minister

Some people have bought into the lie that their leaders are somehow spiritual giants, capable of living the Christian life at a level far beyond their reach. This, they conclude, means that they will never be as effective in sharing the Gospel with others and seeing God touch the lives of others.

This, of course, is complete nonsense! Since you are a priest of God, then wherever you are, whatever sphere of influence you have (and it doesn't matter where that is – it could mean influencing your next door neighbour, someone in the supermarket, in the office, in the factory, in the home – wherever you are), *you* are an ambassador of Jesus Christ and *you* have been called by God to be a priest in that given situation. If only we could just grasp this truth and wake up to its potential, then we could see a move of God in our nation – one that we'd find it hard to even dream about. Jesus only had a team of 12 disciples to work with, but He was able to touch the lives of a vast number of people in just three years. There were only 120 disciples gathered in the upper room on the day of Pentecost, yet 3,000 people were saved in one day when they broke out onto the streets and began to minister. What amazing potential.

The last thing the devil wants is for us to release that potential. He's happy for us to sit in church with our arms folded, nodding and falling asleep now and again. He doesn't want us to fulfil our destiny as a priest and to share the Gospel of Jesus Christ with those whom we come into contact with.

I was told a story by a good friend that I think really illustrates the point that we are all ministers, whether fulltime in the church or in the marketplace of life. He worked in the steel industry and used to go into a pub to complete steel deals every lunchtime. Whilst everyone else was knocking the drink back he would stand there with a tomato juice. One day the barmaid asked him, "How come you only drink tomato juice?" and he said, "Well, I'm a minister and I don't want to be a bad example to the young people." That was all he said, it wasn't a big deal and it marked the end of the conversation.

Three months later he received a phone call just before midnight. A woman was on the other end of the phone and said, "I'm so-and-so's daughter" (she was the barmaid's daughter from his lunchtime pub). "She spoke to you a few months ago. My mother has been taken into hospital – she's dying with cancer. She doesn't know a minister and has asked if you'll go and see her."

So, my friend went to the hospital and led the barmaid to the Lord. Why? Because it was in his sphere of ministry. He was just being himself in the marketplace and allowing God to work through him. Because of this, God used him to bring that woman to a knowledge of saving grace. God can do the same through you because, like my friend, you are a priest, you are a king and God has put you in the world to win people to Jesus.

God will be able to use me more if "x" happens ...

We need to recognise, realise and understand this lie of discouragement. God has put each one of us where we are for a purpose. If you are in a particular job, it is because God has put you there to reach others who work there. He may place you in a specific situation because He has somebody in mind who He wants to reach and you are to be His agent in that task. Maybe you hate your job, however, and spend most of your time wishing that you were someplace else? Maybe you feel that the people you are working with would be totally unreceptive to the Gospel? Maybe, but we still have a duty to share the truth.

Many fall into the trap of saying, "One day, when ...". One day, when I'm in a different job, then I'll feel free to witness to others. One day, when God changes me to be a bit bolder, I'll be sharing the Gospel with everyone I meet, but right now it's just not me ... There are numerous variations on this theme. But instead of making excuses we need to get into our hearts and minds the value of one soul won to Christ. It is worth more to God than the entire world when one person accepts Christ! Wherever we are and whatever we are doing, it is about so much more than simply earning a wage. We are where we are in order to serve God as a priest. This is so important and we really need to understand and accept it.

God has put us here on earth at this moment in time for a reason. The moment we change our attitudes towards the situation God has placed us in is the moment that we will see God begin to move powerfully in that place. By changing our attitude we open the door to invite Jesus into our circumstances, and whenever Jesus shows up miraculous things begin to happen. You are the answer to others people's prayers!

Three types of people

It seems to me that there are three types of people in the Church and how they are affects how they get involved in God's work and to what level they achieve something for His Kingdom. The first two represent reality for many in the Church, but we need to get beyond these and aspire to be the third type of person.

Those who are struggling
The Church must have more struggling people than any organisation on the planet since most people come to church when they're in need of help. They may be struggling emotionally, mentally, physically, financially – in a whole variety of ways. Many people come to the Lord because they've got a problem that they need His help with. Not many people show up at church on a Sunday morning because they've just won the lottery on Saturday! Most people come because they had a need, whether physical or spiritual.

Of course, you can come as you are to God, but you don't have to stay as you are. You can come if you're struggling, but this doesn't mean you should be struggling for the rest of your life. All of us, at some stage, struggle and if I did a survey of any church congregation on a Sunday morning to see how many were, it would be a high percentage. But God does not allow us all to struggle at the same time. That's why we belong to a church, so that those who are strong can help those who are weak. You may be going through a difficult time right now and there will be someone to help you, but by God's grace the time will come when you can help somebody else. This is what the Gospel is all about – that in your struggles you come to Christ and you begin to discover and recognise and realise who you are, who He is and the purpose and plan He's got for your life.

We all struggle at some point, but the problem is many believers have set up camp here, wallowing in their troubles and constantly soaking up the time of other willing Christians who are ministering to them. We need to get real with ourselves and with God, allow Him to deal with our problems, and then move on. We can't remain forever treating the church like a hospital.

Those who live "private" Christian lives

There are those whom God has placed in places of influence (and by that I mean your neighbourhood, your school or college, the factory or shop where you work etc) and you are living your Christian life to the best of your ability, but you don't allow that "life" to spill out and touch others. Some people still subscribe to the view that their faith is a private thing, so nobody else really knows that they are a Christian. Or perhaps they are simply afraid or embarrassed to share their faith?

I've known people who worked together for ten years and neither knew that the other person was a Christian. How can this happen? Because each was keeping the best kept secret in the world and they had made a decision to practice their faith in private. They quietly got on with their lives and let their colleagues get on with theirs.

In the marketplace of life, however, every Christian should be the best they can be in that situation. When we stand before God, all He's going to ask of us is that we did our best with the resources He gave us and acted faithfully. He's not going to demand to know why you didn't witness to as many people as Billy Graham! God simply wants you to be yourself and to witness to the Gospel of Jesus to the best of your ability, whatever situation you happen to be in. We need to be the priests that God has ordained us to be. If you are a salesperson, you should have the best reputation of any of your work colleagues. If you're sweeping part of a factory floor then let your little bit of the floor be the cleanest part of the whole of the factory!

Those who practice biblical principles and change their environment

In any job we should always do our best, of course, because this honours God. When we excel, even in the mundane aspects of life, it builds a platform from which we can speak to others about Christ. Our reputation gives us the right to talk to others about our spiritual life because we have won their respect with our conduct.

We see in the story of Naaman in 2 Kings 5 how a seemingly insignificant person can be used mightily by God to touch the life of another. Naaman was a mighty man of courage. He'd done incredible things and yet the Bible says he was also a leper. He'd taken a captive girl (we don't even know her name) and she was a slave living in his house. She must have been a good servant, a special servant, because when the time came when Naaman realised he was a leper with an incurable disease she was bold enough to be a priest in that situation and say, "Sir, do you know that there is a man that can help you? There's a man you can go to and he will pray for you." It seems obvious to me that she must have been a respected servant in his house for Naaman to listen to her. He listened to what she had to say and then went and was healed of his leprosy, all because this slave girl had such a positive influence. We don't even know her name. She was a servant, a slave, but she was a good servant and a good slave and she earned the right to speak to her master when the moment arose.

That's what authentic Christianity is all about. The time will come when every single person you know will need to know something about God, when sickness suddenly hits them, when death suddenly comes upon their family and all their foundations are shaken and they don't know where to go or what to do. God has put you in their life for that very moment and you will have had to earn the right to be able to tell them exactly what God wants you to say to them. This is what being a minister in the marketplace of life is all about. It's living the Christian life where we are with those whom God has placed us with.

This is authentic Christianity. It's the Gospel in action and is exactly what God has called us to do. It's all about taking Jesus with us wherever we go. It's not about leaving Him in church when we go out and then coming back and picking Him up the following Sunday. It's taking Him where we go! Church was not meant to be an institution that operates just on a Sunday. We *are* the Church. Wherever we are, we are ambassadors of Jesus Christ, chosen by God as kings and priests to take the Gospel to the people. The moment we start doing it we are in for a few surprises because God wants to save people more than they want to be saved.

The Bible says that in the beginning there was the Word and the Word was with God and the Word was God, and the Word became flesh. What we need is for the Word to become flesh in us. It needs to pass from our heads and into our hearts so that we can go out and change the lives of those around us by our example. We need to put away the four lies of discouragement and decide to be people who put their faith into action.

CHAPTER 5

Faith into Action

It's so vitally important that you and I put into practice what we say we believe, because if we don't then there's no point believing it in the first place. We have to be able to express ourselves outside of the safe confines of church. Why bother coming to church if what we do in there does not affect the way we live outside? The main purpose of church is for us to come and be built up, to get encouraged and to be equipped so that when we go out into the mission field God is able to use us to show other people what true Christianity is all about. This is truly exciting.

Most of us probably don't need to hear another sermon because we are already full of biblical teaching. We already have plenty to live off. What we need to do is put what we know into practice so that the Word can become flesh. God's Word must become flesh in you and in me. If only we could begin to practice what we say we believe *and* put it into action, it would take us into a new realm of spiritual life and we would experience an explosion of people becoming born again.

If there are enough people in your church to change your community why isn't it being changed? Remember that Jesus only had twelve disciples! We have far more people in church than Jesus had to work with, yet He and His team still changed their community. Why was this? The simple truth is that the disciples did exactly what Jesus told them to do. I'm only just brave enough to believe there are a few people within the church who will do exactly what Jesus tells them to do and will see what Jesus' disciples saw by way of results.

A key characteristic of authentic Christianity should be the joy of the Lord. Some Christians could do with a double dose of it. Jesus came to give us life in all of its fullness and the Bible says,

> "Do not sorrow, for the joy of the LORD is your strength"
>
> (Nehemiah 8:10)

It is the joy of the Lord that gets me out of bed in the morning and gives me the desire to do His will. If only we could start showing a bit of this joyfulness to others then maybe they would want to know what we've got. There's nothing worse than a miserable Christian. We have to be a real, living advert for the Lord.

Be encouraged

The following are four simple steps to remember when your enthusiasm for sharing the Gospel is ebbing. These are so simple that even I can understand them! It can be quite hard sometimes to find the relevance to your everyday Christian walk in what you hear preached – so called "deep preaching". Sometimes it's best just to keep it simple and to only have the option to say yes or no, so you either do or you don't.

Every occasion is an opportunity to testify

A great friend of mine, Peter Jenkins, shared this story with me:

On the day of the tsunami, Boxing Day 2004, at four o'clock in the morning, Peter received a phone call from Thailand, from a friend called Brian, to tell him what had happened. He turned the television on and, as we all did, followed what was happening as the day unfolded. As his friend was on the phone Peter was given a scripture by God. In Luke 21:11 it says,

> "...there will be great earthquakes in various places, and famines and pestilences; and there will be fearful sights and great signs from heaven"

Then in verse 25 it says,

> "And there will be signs in the sun, in the moon, and in the stars; and on the earth distress of nations, with perplexity, the sea and the waves roaring;"

So, Peter had in Luke 21 a great earthquake with a roaring sea. That's the definition of a tsunami. Jesus prophesied a tsunami: the greatest disaster in history was prophesied as an end time sign. That's pretty amazing.

So Peter thought, "Okay, here is a prophecy being fulfilled" but then right in the middle of Luke 21, verse 13 he saw that it said,

> "But it will turn out for you as an occasion for testimony."

God spoke into his heart that day and said,

"I'm telling you now that every situation can become an opportunity to testify."

Every situation can become an opportunity to testify if only we'll take it. It's there all around us. We don't need to ask God to give us more opportunities, we just need to ask Him to help us take the opportunities that are there.

As a result of what happened in the tsunami the church in Phuket was declared a place of refuge. The church was packed with people who'd lost husbands and wives and had been separated from their family and loved ones by the tsunami. God gave Peter's friend, Brian, a prophetic word that night. He stood in front of all these desperate people and said,

"God has just told me this is a place of miracles and every single person here tonight, within the next twenty-four hours, will find the missing members of their families alive."

Do you know, not one single person in the church that night lost a member of their family in the tsunami. That is totally miraculous. It definitely was an occasion to testify.

"God can take what we perceive as adverse circumstances and turn them around and make them work for us – we just have to be prepared to take the opportunity."

But the testimony didn't stop there: a Swedish family who had been in the church that night went to thank Brian. He humbly said, "Don't thank me, thank my Boss." The Swedish woman went back to Sweden with this in her heart and wrote a book calling it, "Don't thank me, thank my Boss."

This was printed in Sweden, giving full glory to God, the result of an opportunity to testify.

Out of this also came the opportunity to build an orphanage in a village where eighty children had been orphaned by the tsunami. They've now got a nursery and a preschool facility. Following on from that an entire island, a whole tribe, became born again. A school was also rebuilt as a result of the tsunami. When Brian Burton came to visit Solihull, my friend David Carr prophesied over him saying that before the end of the year he would stand before the king in his palace. That happened in the month of May. The following November Brian received a phone call from the palace saying he was being summoned to go and meet the king. The king of Thailand was holding his first meeting since the tsunami because he'd lost his own grandson. Nine hundred people were invited and Brian and Margaret Burton were on the front row because the UK had become the ninth largest country contributing to the tsunami appeal. This in itself was incredible, but Brian was given a medal by the king, one of the highest awards in the whole of Thailand, and was appointed as an advisor to the department of education. Why did all this happen? It was all because Brian took an opportunity to testify. In a country that was 99.8% Buddhist, God took what happened in the tsunami and turned it into an occasion to testify.

God can take what we perceive as adverse circumstances and turn them around and make them work for us – we just have to be prepared to take the opportunity. The moment we speak out, God is on our side. The opportunities are there all the time, but we don't always take them because we don't want to embarrass ourselves. We find it easier to be quiet than to speak. Your prayer shouldn't be "God, give me more opportunities." Your prayer needs to be "God, help me to take the opportunity."

Be a peacemaker

Jesus said,

> "Blessed are the peacemakers, for they shall be called sons of God"
>
> (Matthew 5:9)

Authentic believers need to learn to be peacemakers so that we live like sons of God and offer a true reflection of what God our Father is like.

We've got to learn how to be peacemakers. Sometimes Christians are not peacemakers and instead we are troublemakers. It is known for Christians to sometimes stir up a lot of strife and stress, believe me, but this is totally unbiblical. If we are going to live like children of God we've got to learn to be peace*makers*, not peace*keepers*. A peacekeeper can be a man with a gun! The United Nations send peacekeeping forces into other nations to stop people killing each other and they do so by force. This is not what God is asking of us!

For us to be able to make peace we've got to have peace. When we have the peace of God in us and the peace of God flowing through us, we become a carrier of peace. Isn't this wonderful? As we start to take God's peace into the workplace, into the village, the town, the home, the school, the shop, into the street, then we start living like children of God. Blessed are the peacemakers.

The God of this age has blinded the minds of unbelievers

The Church is too ready to condemn those who do not know Jesus Christ. Yet these unbelievers are blind! We wouldn't dare condemn a blind man for not being able to describe the beauty of a rainbow. And if we were to watch a blind man walk into the road and get hit by a car and we were just standing there doing nothing, what kind of people would that make us? These people are spiritually blind. The God of this age has blinded their minds so they cannot see the light of the Gospel. Therefore, it is not for us to stand in judgement:

> *"And as they went, they entered a village of the Samaritans, to prepare for Him. But they did not receive Him, because His face was set for the journey to Jerusalem. And when His disciples James and John saw this, they said, 'Lord, do You want us to command fire to come down from heaven and consume them, just as Elijah did?' But He turned and rebuked them, and said, 'You do not know what manner of spirit you are of. For the Son of Man did not come to destroy men's lives but to save them.'"*
> (Luke 9:52-54)

We must never condemn people for their spiritual blindness. You know something that they don't and it's up to you to tell them, not in a judgemental or condemning way, but with the grace and peace of the Lord. Don't feel discouraged about how dark the world around you is, instead, take the compassion of Jesus with you and share His good news.

God is sending you!

Here's the good news: God is sending you. He's sending you to those people whose eyes are blind, to open their eyes and to turn them from darkness and from the power of Satan. I don't know about you, but I think that this is fantastic! The people around us are spiritually blind and Jesus is sending us to open their eyes.

Whether it's on the golf course, in a business meeting or whether it's talking to your next door neighbour, Jesus wants to use *you* to open the eyes of somebody who is spiritually blind. Wherever it is, God is sending you there for a purpose because there is somebody waiting for you.

We all know the familiar story of Jesus miraculously feeding a multitude of people. Looking closely at this, we see that the disciples were determined to send the people away, but Jesus wanted to minister to them.

> *"When the day began to wear away, the twelve came and said to Him, 'Send the multitude away, that they may go into the surrounding towns and country, and lodge and get provisions; for we are in a deserted place here.' But He said to them, 'You give them something to eat.'"*
>
> (Luke 9:12-13)

There were five thousand people who needed feeding and what did the disciples say? "Send them away!" They had so missed the point of what Jesus was all about, yet with people like this God managed to build the Church!

> **"Wouldn't it be incredible if every Sunday people piled into churches all over the nation with beaming faces full of joy because they**

had gone into the community and found that everything works in Jesus' name?"

Why did the disciples get confused? Although the crowds needed feeding, the disciples thought it was the wrong place and the wrong time for them to do anything. How many times when God wants us to do something do we think like this? We think to ourselves, not me, not here and not now. In other words, we want God to use somebody else, somewhere else, and at some other time.

There are other examples of where the disciples failed to carry out Jesus' work and misunderstood what was being asked of them:

"Suddenly a man from the multitude cried out, saying, 'Teacher, I implore You, look on my son, for he is my only child. And behold, a spirit seizes him, and he suddenly cries out; it convulses him so that he foams at the mouth; and it departs from him with great difficulty, bruising him. So I implored Your disciples to cast it out, but they could not.'"

(Luke 9:38-40)

There comes a turning point in Luke 10:17, after Jesus had sent seventy people out, when these same disciples who wanted to send the crowd away, who wanted to bring fire down from heaven and who couldn't deal with the demon-possessed returned with *joy*:

"Then the seventy returned with joy, saying, 'Lord, even the demons are subject to us in Your name.'"

They went out, did what was needed and found that it worked.

Wouldn't you like to be able to do this? Wouldn't it be incredible if every Sunday people piled into churches all over the nation with beaming faces full of joy because they had gone into the community and found that everything works in Jesus' name? Imagine the joy we'd return with when even the demons are subject to us in His name. The thought of this is incredible and it is what God wants to do.

Jesus said,

> *"I saw Satan fall from heaven"*
>
> (Luke 10:18)

As you go out doing what Jesus has told you to do, something changes in the spiritual climate. Sometimes when we pray it can feel like the prayers don't go any higher than the ceiling. We've all been there and felt like this.

When Yonggi-Cho, the pastor of the largest church in the world, was asked, "What would you do if you came to Europe? How would you do it? Would you do it the same as you've done it in Korea? Would you set up small cell groups?" do you know what he said? He said, "I'd do nothing, because in Korea I've got an open heaven. In Europe there isn't an open heaven. I'd have to pray and fast and find out from God what the keys and the strategy would be so I could get an open heaven."

When we do what Jesus tells us to do and we start living this kind of life, something happens in the heavenlies; we get a breakthrough. This is what Jesus was saying:

> *"I was watching and I saw Satan fall from heaven like lightning as you went out and did what I was telling you to do, and so there was a breakthrough in the heavenlies and things started to change."*

This is mind-blowing. It's very simple and yet profound so profound that if we can do it we'll see what these disciples saw. They were a miserable lot who wanted to send the people away and wanted to bring fire down, who couldn't deal with the demon-possessed. But we can see what they saw because eventually they did what Jesus told them to do! Jesus said the harvest is plentiful but the labourers are few. How many times have we heard this said? In my church we always need more stewards, especially in the car park. The car park stewards are the most important people in the church because they're the first to greet people and you never get a second chance to make a first impression. We need our best people in the car park! We should not be short of stewards in my church or any church, because we all need to cultivate a servant-heartedness that is prepared to help wherever we are needed. We will struggle to be an example of Jesus by serving others outside the church if we cannot serve Him in the safe environment of our church buildings. Let's start serving in our churches, our homes, and as we start we can learn to take it outside.

Let's draw encouragement from these things and remember, like our friend Brian in the tsunami, every opportunity in life can be a God-opportunity if we will just reach out and grasp it.

CHAPTER 6

Being a Blessing

Authentic Christians are a blessing to others and we feel good whenever we are around them because they exude the presence of Christ. Jesus taught His disciples the practice of "taking His peace" with them into the homes of others. "When you enter a home," He said, "say 'peace' to that house." In other words, we should be a blessing to people.

We all need all the blessings we can get. Wouldn't you be glad if somebody came to visit you in your house and when they left you felt blessed? Wouldn't you be glad they'd been in your house? We may not like doing door-to-door evangelism and many will feel that it isn't suitable in today's society, but it is a great way to bless people.

> **"God wants us to be carriers of His blessing. When we step out and do what the Lord tells us to do to bless others we are always in for an exciting time."**

The people who are doing door-to-door work are the people who are building new churches everywhere. Why? Because there are people in those houses crying out for somebody to come and speak to them, for somebody to come and show them some love and support.

It should be the case that, if we are true children of God, when we go into somebody's house we take the blessing of God with us. You should be blessed because you've been with me and I should be blessed because I've been with you, and we all should be blessed because we've been with Jesus. It isn't very complicated!

We have been called to be a blessing:

"I will bless you and make your name great; And you shall be a blessing."

(Genesis 12:2)

This is what God said to Abraham. It doesn't end with us being blessed; the finishing line is for us to be the blessing. God wants us to be carriers of His blessing. When we step out and do what the Lord tells us to do to bless others we are always in for an exciting time. Jesus is the joy of living. When we start becoming carriers of the blessing of God then people are glad to be in our presence.

The word "blessed" can be used as an acronym for what it really means to put blessing into practice.

B – Body
Jesus came to save that which was lost. The Gospel of Jesus Christ is for the whole man, *body*, soul, mind and spirit. In order to bless others we can pray for physical healing so that their body might be made whole.

L – Labour
In the work environment today, where people's jobs are no longer secure, we can pray blessing over their businesses, blessing over their places of work. Start praying for your bosses. Instead of moaning about them, pray for them. If you are the boss then don't forget to pray for your staff.

E – Emotions

"But the fruit of the Spirit is love, joy, peace, longsuffering, kindness, goodness, faithfulness, gentleness, self-control."

(Galatians 5:22-23)

We can administer love, joy and peace. These are fruits of the Spirit. If we have the Holy Spirit living in us and we are carriers of His presence, then we can bless people emotionally.

S – Social relationships

We have to cultivate and nourish good relationships with those around us. Therefore we should spend time with people, talking and praying, so we can to truly understand where we can be a blessing in their lives.

We also have to reach out to those in our social circles who we would naturally avoid. Remember the words of Jesus:

"But I say to you who hear: Love your enemies, do good to those who hate you, bless those who curse you, and pray for those who spitefully use you."

(Luke 6:27-28)

S – Salvation

I like to recall the Good News of Salvation from Isaiah 61 as a reminder as to why I'm called to be a blessing to others.

"The Spirit of the Lord GOD is upon Me,
  Because the LORD has anointed Me
  To preach good tidings to the poor;
  He has sent Me to heal the brokenhearted,

> To proclaim liberty to the captives,
> And the opening of the prison to those who are bound;"
>
> (Isaiah 61:1)

E – Evangelism

In this era of false doctrine and teaching we have to speak the true Word of God more than ever before. It is the will of God.

> *"Preach the word! Be ready in season and out of season. Convince, rebuke, exhort, with all longsuffering and teaching. For the time will come when they will not endure sound doctrine, but according to their own desires, because they have itching ears, they will heap up for themselves teachers; and they will turn their ears away from the truth, and be turned aside to fables. But you be watchful in all things, endure afflictions, do the work of an evangelist, fulfil your ministry."*
>
> (2 Timothy 4:2-5)

D – Discipleship

The word disciple translates as "learner". A true disciple is someone who walks in God's ways and learns from His teachings. We need to constantly learn the ways of Jesus in order to be efficient in our blessing of others. It's also much easier to minister to the needs of those around you when you follow God's will and understand what is required. As we saw in Chapter 5 there were occasions where the disciples often missed the needs of the people. So, if we look to the Bible for our lead we will find all that's needed to be a blessing.

A shining light

Often we want to preach to people before we've even earned the right to speak to them. We've got to allow them to see what we do before they'll open their ears to us and hear what we say. Let your good works be seen and let your light be seen. What did Jesus say?

> *"Let your light so shine before men, that they may see your good works and glorify your Father in heaven."*
> (Matthew 5:16)

Billy Graham said, "Lighthouses don't ring bells or sound sirens, they just shine." That's all they do – they shine. Electricity doesn't make any noise, but it has the power to produce light. Before we say anything, let's earn the right to say it. People have got to see what we do before they'll hear what we have to say. It's very important and what blessing others is all about.

Fellowship

As we go into a situation and bless people the next stage is to have fellowship with them. Yes, I'm telling you to spend time with non-Christians. This is exactly what Jesus did. Those around Him accused Him of being a friend of sinners. I don't mind being called a friend of sinners because I believe it's the best thing you could ever accuse me of! It is a direct comparison to how Jesus lived. He spent time, after all, with the people who the religious people wouldn't spend time with. If we want to have the opportunity to tell them about Jesus then we've got to spend time with them wherever they're at. This is what Jesus taught.

One of the worst things you can do is to go into somebody's house and then, when they offer you something to eat, to refuse food because you don't like it. This is a huge conversation stopper. You have to be sensitive to their customs and expectations and pray and get on with it. Remember, obedience and sacrifice! Bless them and eat some food with them. It's a brilliant opportunity and there's never a better environment to have discussion than over a meal.

When Jesus was with His disciples the Last Supper was not just a bit of wafer and a sip of wine. The meal lasted for hours as they sat down and celebrated Passover. It was a full-blown feast. If we want to win people for Jesus and bless them then maybe we've got to be prepared to spend a bit more time with them. Whatever they give to you, eat it. I'll pray over it and then go home and eat the antacids if I have to!

In my church we had an outreach in a local park amongst a community with a high Asian, West Indian and Afro-Caribbean population. It's was like a carnival. We prayed for a way to get people to come to our Asian church on Sundays and God gave us the words, "A little child will lead you."

Because of this we got the name of the church, Sanctuary, printed onto balloons. Our gazebo was giving out free balloons for all the children with the kids dragging their parents to our tent to get one. When they received a balloon they were also given an invite to come to church on Sunday where we were dishing up free curry. God had a plan and gave us this strategy. Sometimes we can make it too complicated and deliberate for too long until we've missed our chance. All this took was free balloons!

So, bless people. Eat and drink what they put before you and fellowship with them. Build relationships with them. When you do this, this simple thing, the opportunity to minister to their needs opens up.

The key is peace

When you take time to develop relationships with people they begin to trust you and then begin to see that you really do care. Contrary to expectations, you're not just a fly-by-night so they begin to share their needs. You are there to minister to those needs. You're there to be the ambassador of Christ, to be a priest, to be a king and to minister.

You have to wait for that moment when a person opens up their heart and begins to share with you. The Bible says that God wants all people to have His peace:

> *"I urge, then, first of all, that requests, prayers, intercession and thanksgiving be made for everyone—for kings and all those in authority, that we may live peaceful and quiet lives in all godliness and holiness. This is good, and pleases God"*
> (1 Timothy 2:1-3 NIV)

Do you want to please God? If so, be a carrier of peace. Take God's peace into the homes and into the places where people are: the work environment, the college, factory and home. Take the peace of God with you and bless the people.

You may be the only Christian in your home. When you are there you must take and keep God's peace with you. Be a blessing in your home.

You're the first Christian and as you begin to change your attitude you'll begin to be a blessing in your home. You'll find that members of your family will even begin to open up to you about stuff that you never even knew before. This gives you an opportunity to minister to their needs.

"Bless people, fellowship with people, minister to people and proclaim the Gospel.

Tell all that the kingdom of God is coming. This isn't complicated."

By God's grace we have to do this in the church and try to help people practically. Don't cut back on giving to the poor! When we give to the poor God will always take care of us. You need to understand this and the Bible is full of it.

> *"Then Jesus, looking at him, loved him, and said to him, 'One thing you lack: Go your way, sell whatever you have and give to the poor, and you will have treasure in heaven; and come, take up the cross, and follow Me.'"*
> (Mark 10:21)

When people come with their needs the church should minister into those needs practically and also pray for and with them. I don't know many people who say no when you ask if you can pray for them. In my experience very few people say no to it.

The good news

The psalmist wrote,

> *"Sing to the LORD, bless His name;*
> *Proclaim the good news of His salvation from day to day.*
> *Declare His glory among the nations,*
> *His wonders among all peoples."*
> (Psalm 96:2-3)

As we begin to develop our relationships and fellowship with other people, and as we begin to minister into the needs and share with them in a practical way, we have paved the way to be able tell them about the Kingdom of God. We can declare the good news of His salvation and declare His glory to them. By ministering to their needs we have earned the right to tell them that the Kingdom of God is coming. When we tell them about Jesus we can stand back and watch the results. Remember, the seventy returned with great joy – the same bunch that wanted to send the crowd away! These were the same people who wanted to bring fire down and who couldn't even deal with the demons. They rejoiced and came back saying, "Lord! It works! Even the demons are subject unto your name!"

Bless people, fellowship with people, minister to people and proclaim the Gospel. Tell all that the kingdom of God is coming. This isn't complicated. It's no good just blessing a hungry person; we've got to feed them and satisfy their practical needs and then get ready to tell them that the Kingdom of God has come. We can tell them that Jesus is waiting for them to open up their lives and their hearts to receive Him because of what He did on the cross.

Encouragement

I want to give you some encouragement, some simple steps to remember when you're struggling to find the will of God in your life and bless those around you. If a person encourages you it can just mean so much and so I would like to share the following as a blessing to you.

I let these following four questions form four lines of a box. I try to live my life inside this box because it gives me all the security I could ever want. The answers to these questions give me identity, purpose and every reason for living my life:

Is there a God?
Yes!

Does God care?
God cares for us so much that He gave His only Son, Jesus, who died for us. But does He care for *you*? That's the big issue so we draw the next line of the box.

Does He care for me?

> "Therefore humble yourselves under the mighty hand of God, that He may exalt you in due time, casting all your care upon Him, for He cares for you."
>
> (1 Peter 6-7)

Does God have a plan for my life?
Yes, for every single person. God Almighty saw you, even in your mother's womb, and the Bible says that every day has been written in the book. I truly believe this for,

> "This is the day the LORD has made; We will rejoice and be glad in it"
>
> (Psalm 118:24)

The thing is, we've got to discover this plan as most of us never fully discover what God has in store for us. We muddle through life as Christians and we hope that when we die we're going to go to Heaven and that's the whole purpose of it.

Thank God that we believe we have this inheritance beyond the grave. However, I still believe that God has something for us to do right *now*, today, here on Earth. This week could be the most exciting week in the history of the Church. All it requires is for every single one of us doing what God wants us to do, saying what He wants us to say, being what He wants us to be and going where He wants us to go. In short, God wants us to be authentic Christians and follow in the footsteps of His Son, Jesus Christ.

Do not just base your Christian faith on the spiritual experiences you have in church. Instead, base it upon the Word of God, the only thing that can make us true followers of Christ.

"Finally, all of you be of one mind, having compassion for one another; love as brothers, be tenderhearted, be courteous; not returning evil for evil or reviling for reviling, but on the contrary blessing, knowing that you were called to this, that you may inherit a blessing."

(1 Peter 3:8)

Authentic or Synthetic Christianity?

CHAPTER 7

Suppose you go to the doctor and learn that you have an advanced case of breast cancer. What would you think if the oncologist, after giving you the diagnosis, just smiled at you, said he understood your problem, gave you a placebo and said, "Just go and take this once a day for three months and everything will be all right"? Do you think you will love that doctor for how he is treating your disease? No, you should find another doctor!

Yet this is exactly what is happening in the evangelical world where the issue is not breast cancer, but the most severe disease possible: the sin that separates man from God. In the Gospel God has given us a prescription and the only medicine powerful enough to save us from sin. The Bible says that the

> "Gospel is the power of God unto salvation to everyone who believes,"

but in many churches, preachers refuse to preach the Gospel. "Speak to us soft, smooth things!" the people say, and when the minister does so, they are happy. How many people go to such churches just to have their spirits massaged and go home thinking they are saved! But nothing is really happening to them and they are not saved, because they have not even heard the true Gospel!

Let's examine the apostolic definition of an authentic Christian. There is a Christianity that is synthetic. Synthetic Christianity is popular, but it is counterfeit and a placebo, not real medicine. Synthetic Christianity is based on mere profession of God and a mental assent to a set of theological propositions. But mere profession and mental assent will not save anyone. The Bible tells us that demons believe and tremble. In fact, it was a demon who first confessed that Jesus is the Christ, the Son of God, long before Peter or anyone else made that profession.

A synthetic Christian is one who says, "I am a Christian because I received Jesus into my life as Saviour. Because I made a decision for Christ, I am saved and it doesn't matter what I do." Although Scripture teaches that the grace and forgiveness of God is always available for us if we come to Him in true repentance, we should not live our lives like that. It does matter what we do! Our aim should be to cooperate with the Holy Spirit so that our lives are transformed from the inside out and we now behave differently.

Rather than saying they are saved to sin no more, some people argue (not necessarily verbally, but by their actions) that they are saved to sin even more, claiming grace as their immunity. But this is the kind of Christianity that the apostle Paul condemned and referred to as a brand of religion that "only has the form of godliness but denies its power." Such people have not become a new creation in Christ and have not been given a new heart with which they can obey God. They profess to be Christians, but in practice are no different to unbelievers. They are only fooling themselves.

Tests of Authentic Christianity

In the first epistle of John, the apostle gives a definition of authentic Christianity and an authentic Christian. John says that a true Christian is born of God and therefore has a new heart — a heart of flesh, not of stone. Because a Christian has a new heart, he also has a new intellect, a new mind, a new will, and new emotions.

In 1 John 5:1 we read,

> *"Everyone who believes that Jesus is the Christ is born of God."*

One who is born of God has a new mind and will make the correct, orthodox confession that Jesus is the Christ. Why does a Christian have a new mind? He has been born of God. So this confession made with his intellect is the result of supernatural regeneration.

In 1 John 2:29 we read,

> *"If you know that he is righteous, you know that everyone who does what is right has been born of him."*

This means the person who obeys God and does righteousness has been born of God. His obedience proves that he has received a new will because he experienced the great miracle of God called regeneration.

Not only does an authentic Christian have a new intellect and new will, but he also has new affections, new emotions. In 1 John 4:7 we read,

> *"Dear friends, let us love one another, for love comes from God. Everyone who loves has been born of God and knows God."*

> **"Synthetic Christianity is popular,
> but it is counterfeit and a placebo,
> not real medicine."**

A Christian loves God. He has this new affection, new emotion by which he loves God because he has been born of God. So our confession that Jesus Christ is Lord is not a self-generated confession, but the direct result of our new birth. A person who is born of God is a new creation. If we are regenerate, our mind, will, and affections have all been made new by God.

What is the result of a person's mind, will, and emotions being made new by God? Such a person will now think God's thoughts with his intellect and study God's Word so that he can know it. Such a person will "will" God's will. In other words he will want to obey God and do His will. Such a person will love God and others because his affections have been made new.

If we love God and his people, then we are authentic Christians. John taught this, as did the apostle Paul, who wrote about it in 1 Corinthians 13. There we read in verses 1-3,

> *"If I speak in the tongues of men and of angels, but have not love, I am only a resounding gong or a clanging cymbal. If I have the gift of prophecy and can fathom all mysteries and all knowledge, and if I have a faith that can move mountains, but have not love, I am nothing. If I give all I possess to the poor and surrender my body to the flames but have not love, I gain nothing."*

What is Love?

What is the nature of the love John is speaking about? In these six verses, 1 John 4:7-12, the "love" word group, including the words *agapê*, *agapaô*, *agapêtos*, appears fourteen times. The world has no understanding of *agapê* love. The world only really knows a love called *eros*. Eros asks the question, "What can I get out of this relationship for my personal gain?" In other words, *eros* is self-centeredness. Thus, the world knows love only in the context of lust, possession and gain.

But the love that John spoke about, which is expressed by the Greek word *agapê*, is not the love of this world. This world does not know what *agapê* love is because it is not of this sinful, fallen world. *Agapê* love is heavenly love.

So John wrote in verse 7,

"Dear friends, let us love one another, for love comes from God."

Agapê love does not come from this world nor from the devil nor from sinful men. *Agapê* love comes from God. *Agapê* love is an expression of the nature of God. So it is *agapê*, not *eros*, that is the very eternal nature of God. This love is a giving love. It asks, "How much can I give to the other?" though the other is utterly undeserving. This divine, giving love is the polar opposite of the love of this world called *eros*.

Let us then look at God's love especially as it has been displayed in and through the person of his Son. God the Father sent from heaven the greatest gift He possessed: His Son, who is eternal, preexistent, and co-equal with the Father. What a demonstration of God's great love for us!

God could have given no greater gift than His only beloved Son. In Jesus Christ God gave us the best, the greatest, the grandest gift that heaven possessed.

In Romans 8:32 Paul says that God, *"did not spare his own Son ..."* meaning His eternal, beloved, unique, one and only Son. Isaac, Abraham's only son, was spared, and other sons have been spared as well. But the infinite God did not spare His Son, but gave Him up for us all. Divine love gives the best.

We are told that God "sent" His Son. This means God sent His beloved Son with a mission, with a responsibility, with work to do. He was to fulfill this mission by His incarnation.

What humiliation for the Son of God to come into this world of sin, of sinners, of poverty, of misery, of enmity and contradiction, and to be conceived in the womb of a woman, born of a woman, have no place in the inn, be placed in a manger, and to be mocked, contradicted and crucified on our behalf. Jesus humbled Himself, not only to become incarnate, but to die on the cross. That is love.

What was the purpose of God's sending His Son into the world?

"That we might live through him."

The Purpose of God's Love

The Bible tells us we are sinners—spiritually dead and under the wrath of God. In Romans 5 we read something about those whom God loved. In verse 6 Paul wrote,

"You see, just at the right time, when we were still powerless, Christ died for the ungodly."

By nature we are ungodly. We are powerless to save ourselves, powerless to improve ourselves, and powerless to make ourselves acceptable to God. Paul continued,

"Very rarely will anyone die for a righteous man, though for a good man someone might possibly dare to die. But God demonstrates his own love for us in this: while we were still sinners, Christ died for us."

Not only were we powerless and ungodly, but we were sinners. And in verse 10 Paul wrote that we were enemies of God as well:

"For if when we were God's enemies we were reconciled to him through the death of his Son, how much more, having been reconciled, shall we be saved through his life."

In Romans 8:7 Paul wrote,

"The sinful mind is hostile to God."

You see, God loved us, though we were undeserving, without strength, ungodly sinners at enmity with Him. Every religion, every philosophy, and everything else in this world is by nature "against God" and views God as being against them. Paul wrote,

"The sinful mind is hostile to God. It does not submit to God's law nor can it do so."

It is impossible for a sinful man to submit to God's law. Finally, in verse 8 he wrote,

> *"Those controlled by the sinful nature cannot please God."*

Supernatural regeneration is absolutely essential for salvation so that we may submit to God's law and please God.

Because we are by nature ungodly sinners, without strength and at enmity with God, what happens to us? In Romans 1:18 we read,

> *"The wrath of God is being revealed from heaven against all the godlessness and wickedness of men."*

God is angry against the unbelieving sinful world. Yet God sent His Son that we may have life through Him. This means the people in this world do not live, in the true sense of living. They exist, but they do not live because they are cut off from God by their own sin. But God sent His Son into this world of sin that we may finally live.

In 1 John 5:11-12 we read,

> *"And this is the testimony: God has given us eternal life, and this life is in his Son."*

Here we see that all other religions and philosophies and all other ways of finding eternal life and salvation are absolutely false. In other words, either all other religions and philosophies are right or God is right in His Word. The apostolic doctrine declares that God has given us eternal life through His Son. I would rather believe in God and His apostolic testimony than anything else.

John writes,

> *"And this is the testimony ..."*

Whose testimony is it? God's.

> *"This is the testimony: God has given us eternal life and this life is in his Son. He who has the Son has life."*

We cannot find eternal life outside of Jesus Christ. Life is found only in Him, and only He can give us life. In John 10:10 Jesus Christ said,

> *"The thief comes only to steal and kill and destroy; I have come that they may have life, and have it to the full."*

Satan's goal is to destroy people, and he does so through any means. Even while some people go to church, they are being destroyed by Satan. Such people, who trust in their puny little intellects, have no life. Theirs is mere existence, cut off from God. I pray that such people will repent and trust in Christ alone, in whom alone is found abundant eternal life.

In 1 John 4:10 we read,

> *"This is love: not that we loved God, but that he loved us and sent his Son as an atoning sacrifice for our sins."*

Jesus Christ, God's one and only eternal Son, humbled Himself and became incarnate so that He could, as the great High Priest, offer to God the bloody, acceptable sacrifice of Himself. He did so in accordance with God's own eternal plan, so that God's just wrath against us could be turned away so that He could be gracious to us and forgive us all our sins.

The wrath of God against us has been poured out on a substitute: His only Son, the God/man Jesus Christ. That is what love is all about. Our Lord Jesus Christ became our substitute, taking upon Himself the entirety of the wrath of God that we merited and deserved. The eternal Son became both the victim and the priest. As we read in 2 Corinthians 5:21,

> *"God made him who knew no sin be sin for us, so that in him we might become the righteousness of God."*

Jesus Christ was cursed so that we who were cursed may be blessed forever.

God the Father sent his Son into the world to the death of the cross. That is what love is all about. As John wrote in 1 John 1:7,

> *"The blood of Jesus, his Son, purifies us from all sin."*

This is the highest manifestation of divine *agapê* love. It is not mere sentiment or words. I have heard people making many promises and not keeping them. Such people are false, they are liars. God not only makes promises but He fulfills them. The entire Old Testament is God's promise and because God is not a man that he should lie, in the fullness of time, He displayed His love by sending His Son into this world to die on the cross.

In 1 Peter 1:18-19 we read,

> *"For you know that it was not with perishable things such as silver and gold that you were redeemed from the empty way of life handed down to you from your forefathers, but with the precious blood of Christ ..."*

God Himself bought us back from slavery to sin, Satan, death, and hell, by paying the price of His Son, *"a lamb without blemish and defect."*

In Colossians 1:14 Paul wrote,

"In him we have redemption, the forgiveness of sins,"

...meaning the complete full pardon and forgiveness of all our sins. That is what love is all about.

Notice the word "so" in John 3:16. God *so* loved the world. This "so" means the person and the work of Christ for miserable, wretched enemies of God. This is what love is all about. No one can measure its height, its depth, its breadth. We can try to know it, but as Paul tells us in Ephesians 3, the knowledge of God's love is incomprehensible. No one can understand this amazing grace and amazing love in all its fullness except God Himself.

According to the biblical definition, then, an authentic Christian is *one who loves God*. True love is the expression of God's nature, because God Himself is love. God revealed this love in history by so loving the world that He sent His Son, the Lord Jesus Christ, into the world

"that whoever believes in him shall not perish but have eternal life."

That speaks about the person of Christ, about the work of Christ, and about us who merited the very wrath of God, and yet to whom God showed mercy.

God, who is love, showed His love to us through the person and work of His Son, Jesus Christ. But Jesus, after he died and rose again, ascended into heaven and is now seated as King of kings at the right hand of God the Father. He is not here; He has risen! But if Jesus Christ is in heaven, how can God's love be revealed to the world? The answer is that

He who is love, He who showed us His love in Jesus Christ, still demonstrates His love in and through the Christian and the Christian community. In other words, God expresses His love to the world through the life and actions of every authentic Christian.

※ ※

The challenge each of us faces is to live out our faith in a real, living and vibrant way, anchored on the love of Christ and expressing that love to a broken, hurting world. I included the exegesis on love from Scripture above because it reminds us who we are, whose we are, and what has been invested in us – not purely for our own benefit, even though it is life-transforming for us, but for the benefit of others, those who are lost and outside of Christ. This is the message of the Gospel and this is *authentic Christianity*, the real deal.

About the author

Richard is an author, presenter, and pastor and founder of the *Gateway Foundation* and Director of Victory Outreach UK.

He is in great demand as a speaker at conferences and churches and also in secular life as a public/motivational speaker. He has presented for the BBC, and appears on numerous radio and TV programmes as an expert guest.

As well as his public appearances he is author of *Positive Power*, *Making your Faith Work*, and his autobiography *To Catch a Thief* has sold thousands of copies and been translated into a number of other languages. His book has also been placed into prisons throughout the UK and in 2008 won the book of the year award.

Richard is married to Jill and they have 4 sons Joshua, Caleb, Jacob and Isaac.

Visit www.richardtaylor.org.uk for more information and contact details.

See also www.vouk.org.uk for information on Richard's work with Victory Outreach UK.

We hope you enjoyed reading this New Wine book.
For details of other New Wine books
and a wide range of titles from other
Word and Spirit publishers visit our website:
www.newwineministries.co.uk
or e mail us at newwine@xalt.co.uk